Data Management and Analysis Using JMP®

Health Care Case Studies

Jane E. Oppenlander • Patricia Schaffer

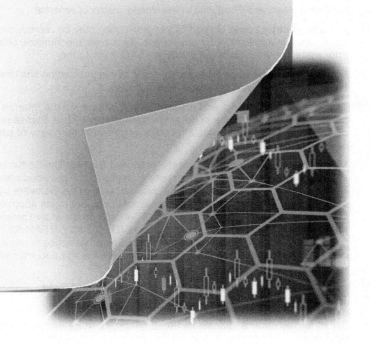

sas.com/books

The correct bibliographic citation for this manual is as follows: Oppenlander, Jane E., and Patricia Schaffer. 2017. *Data Management and Analysis Using JMP®: Health Care Case Studies*. Cary, NC: SAS Institute Inc.

Data Management and Analysis Using JMP®: Health Care Case Studies

Contents

About This Book

Purpose

Data Management and Analysis Using JMP: Health Care Case Studies bridges the gap between the traditional first statistics course and the successful application of statistical analysis in the workplace. It illustrates a holistic, step-by-step approach to analyzing health care data, showing practitioners and students how to solve real-world problems by example. We employ a problem-solving strategy that includes problem definition, data management, a framework for selecting analysis methods, step-by-step JMP instructions, and how to interpret statistical results in context.

The cases begin by illustrating techniques to prepare data for analysis, followed by applying appropriate statistical methods to explore and analyze the data, and, finally, disseminate results to stakeholders. The statistical analysis methods covered are the foundational techniques commonly applied to meet regulatory, operational, budgeting, and research needs in the health care industry. Groups of cases are organized around different scenarios and data sets and illustrate a logical progression for problem solving, beginning with data visualization and descriptive analysis and continuing to statistical inference and model building. Much of the data is open-source, drawn from a variety of health care settings.

Is This Book for You?

Data Management and Analysis Using JMP: Health Care Case Studies is designed for beginner and intermediate JMP users who are working or studying in health care fields. It is appropriate as either a textbook or supplement for an introductory statistics course focusing on health care applications. The cases and associated exercises can be used for classroom activities or for self-study. This book can also serve as a useful reference for working professionals in health care fields.

Prerequisites

This casebook assumes the reader has taken an introductory statistics course and has basic navigational facility with JMP.

Scope of This Book

This casebook covers basic data management techniques suitable for preparing data for analysis. JMP's data visualization capabilities, invaluable for exploring and presenting data, are included in each case. Statistical methods traditionally covered in introductory statistics courses are presented, including descriptive analysis, univariate and bivariate statistical inference, and simple and multiple regression analysis.

About the Examples

Software Used to Develop the Book's Content

JMP® 13 was used in the cases presented in this book.

Example Code and Data

The data files that accompany our cases can be downloaded from the authors' pages at https://www.sas.com/sas/books/authors/jane-oppenlander.html or https://www.sas.com/sas/books/authors/patricia-schaffer.html.

Output and Graphics Used in This Book

The cases give step-by-step instructions for solving problems using JMP. The relevant JMP dialogs and output are shown in each case.

Exercise Solutions

Instructors can request solutions to the exercises by writing to saspress@sas.com.

Additional Resources

Additional case studies can be downloaded from the JMP Case Study Library (www.jmp.com). These cover topics such as health care and quality improvement, statistics and biostatistics, analytics and predictive modeling, and business statistics.

The following resources provide more detailed explanations of data management, visualization, and analysis methods:

Cleveland, William S., *The Elements of Graphing Data*, 2nd ed., Hobart Press, 1994.

DAMA International, *DAMA Guide to the Data Management Body of Knowledge*, 2nd ed., Technics Press, 2017.

Few, Stephen, *Show Me the Numbers: Designing Tables and Graphs to Enlighten*, 2nd ed., Analytics Press, 2012.

Fowler, F. J., Jr., *Survey Research Methods*, 5th ed., Sage Publications, 2013.

Polit, D. F., *Statistics and Data Analysis for Nursing Research*, 2nd ed., Pearson, 2010.

Rossner, B., *Fundamentals of Biostatistics*, 8th ed., Cengage Learning, 2015.

Tufte, Edward R., *The Visual Display of Quantitative Information*, 2nd ed., Graphics Press, 2001.

Keep in Touch

We look forward to hearing from you. We invite questions, comments, and concerns. If you want to contact us about a specific book, please include the book title in your correspondence.

To Contact the Author through SAS Press

By e-mail: saspress@sas.com

Via the Web: http://support.sas.com/author_feedback

SAS Books

For a complete list of books available through SAS, visit http://www.sas.com/books.

Phone: 1-800-727-3228

Fax: 1-919-677-8166

E-mail: sasbook@sas.com

Learn About New SAS Press Books

Sign up for our new book announcements--and receive exclusive discounts! Subscribe to the SAS New Books monthly email here: http://support.sas.com/newbooks

Publish with SAS

SAS is recruiting authors! Are you interested in writing a book? Visit www.sas.com/publish for more information.

About the Authors

Jane E. Oppenlander is a professor at Clarkson University, where she teaches statistics for the School of Business and the Clarkson University-Ichan School of Medicine at Mount Sinai Bioethics Program. She has more than 30 years of experience applying statistics and operations research in the energy industry. Jane is a certified Six Sigma Master Black Belt. A long-time JMP and SAS user, she received her Ph.D. in Administrative and Engineering Systems from Union College in Schenectady, New York.

Patricia Schaffer is President of Total Quality Associates, Inc., a New York-based consulting firm. Pat has worked with private and public sector information systems for over 30 years with a concentration in the design, development, implementation, and quality assurance of data warehouse and master data management solutions. She also held the position of adjunct professor of Management Information Systems at Union Graduate College in Schenectady, NY.

Acknowledgments

We thank Marilyn Stapleton of the Ellis Medicine - Belanger School of Nursing for providing the nursing survey data and for her insights into the practice of nursing and health care research. The suggestions of the technical reviewers were invaluable for improving our cases. We are especially appreciative of the efforts of Brant Deppa, Dean Poeth, and Eva Williford. Mia Stephens and Ruth Hummel provided detailed and insightful comments that greatly improved the introduction. Our thanks also to Mary Ann Shifflet, Shirley Smerling, Eric Stephens, Amy Cohen, and Susan Madden for their encouragement and helpful comments. We gratefully acknowledge the many students at Clarkson University and Union Graduate College who pilot-tested these cases and offered valuable feedback.

The staff of SAS Press has been most helpful through this project. We thank book cover designer Robert Harris, technical publishing specialists Monica McClain and Denise T. Jones, and copy editor Lauree Shepard. Lastly, we are indebted to Stacey Hamilton for her enthusiasm, hard work, and guidance throughout this project.

1

Introduction

Data Analysis in Health Care

Data acquisition and analysis is now pervasive throughout the health care industry. Researchers developing new medical devices, pharmaceuticals, and treatment protocols employ rigorous study designs and statistical methods. Public health personnel collect data when investigating disease outbreaks and disseminate health statistics and risks to the general public through awareness campaigns to improve population health. Administrators of health care organizations collect and analyze data to support decisions involving resource allocation and to assess the quality of care and utilization of services. Clinicians make patient treatment choices using evidence-based practice.

The advent of electronic medical records, government mandates for data capture and reporting, and the ability to collect and store massive amounts of data has enabled the application of analytics to real-life health care problems. Personnel at all levels and functions of health care organizations are producers and consumers of data and analysis with the goal of containing health care costs and improving patient care.

Problem Solving Framework

The cases in this book are designed to assist those in the health care field seeking to address practical problems. In introductory statistics courses the basic concepts are often taught using clearly defined problems and well-organized data sets with a focus on executing statistical techniques. Our cases extend the basic application of statistical methods to a more holistic approach which will assist practitioners in coping with the "messiness" found in real-life problems and data. Effective presentation of data and statistical results is key to driving change that will improve health care delivery.

A useful framework for addressing data-driven problems is the 1/3, 1/3, 1/3 guideline. Aim to spend 1/3 of your time preparing for analysis, 1/3 of your time on analysis, and 1/3 of your time summarizing and disseminating your results. Figure 1.1 on page 2 illustrates this problem-solving process.

Figure 1.1   *Problem Solving Framework – The 1/3, 1/3, 1/3 Guideline*

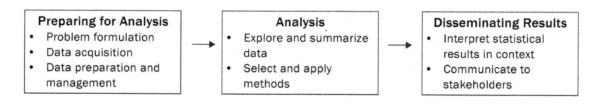

Each problem you encounter will be different and the actual amount of time you spend may not be equal for all three steps. To have an impact, analysis results must be communicated in ways that are meaningful to stakeholders and guide actions that yield improved service delivery. The strength of an analysis depends on a clearly specified problem statement and on the quality of the data. Rushing any of these steps jeopardizes the quality of the next step and can ultimately reduce stakeholder confidence in the conclusions.

Preparing for Analysis

Problem Formulation

Problems arise in health care from the desire to increase efficiency, contain costs, improve the quality of care, and seek new clinical knowledge. All too often, data is collected and analysis is begun on problems that are ill-posed. This inevitably results in rework, frustrated stakeholders, project delays, and wasted resources. Time spent on developing a clear, complete problem statement is time well spent. Initially, many requests for data analysis are the result of an idea or question that is not fully thought through. A good first step is to write the problem down as you understand it and have stakeholders review it. Once you have incorporated all of their comments and are satisfied that you have captured the problem correctly, you will need to get consensus from all stakeholders before proceeding. Several iterations may be required until the problem is properly captured.

Central to the problem statement is the research question, which is a concise statement of the desired inquiry. A research question must be specific so that data can be obtained and analyzed to answer the question. For example, "what is a good hospital stay?" is not specific enough. What must be specified are the characteristics of a "good" hospital stay (e.g., quality of care, cost, food, condition of the facility) and from whose perspective (e.g., patient, clinician, insurer). From the research question, the data needed can be identified and the appropriate statistical methods selected. Everything rests on the problem statement and research question.

Consider the following example. A hospital board has set a goal of improving patient satisfaction of hospital stay while maintaining quality care and keeping costs low. A patient survey is initiated to first assess current patient satisfaction. The survey will address patient satisfaction with overall quality of care, overall cost to the patient, food quality, and condition of the facility. In addition to Likert-scale ratings questions, the survey will also include some choice model questions to determine patients' priorities in the various potential improvement areas. For example, "Which of the following is more important to you: improvements in overall cost, improvements in qualifications/training/prestige of health care professionals, or improvements in patient comfort?" At the conclusion of this survey phase, the board will identify the areas of poor patient satisfaction and will rank these according to patient prioritization. In the second phase of this study, the board will propose potential improvements for the identified areas, and will investigate the costs associated with these changes. A recommendation report will be drafted and presented to the hospital administration.

Data Acquisition

Once the problem statement is complete, data must be obtained that can be analyzed to address the research question. There are three choices: collect the data, use existing data, or combine both.

Data can be collected by an experiment, observation, or survey. Such studies must be carefully designed in order to obtain high quality data and can require considerable time, effort and funding. When human subjects are involved, approvals must be obtained from an institutional review board. Studies are designed to generate the data that will meet the needs of your specific problem.

Data from an existing source may be quickly obtained but since it was not generated for your specific purpose, additional processing may be needed. An additional concern when using existing sources is the quality of the data and the potential for bias based on how the data was collected. When using existing data, strive to obtain data from reputable, independent sources. For example, if you are studying mortality due to gun violence, data from a government or independent organization is preferable to that from a political or special interest group. When using existing data, understanding the study design and conditions under which the data was obtained is often needed to select appropriate statistical methods.

The manner in which you acquire data, either by collecting it yourself or obtaining it from someone else, will depend on the problem, your project timeline, and the resources available. If the cost to obtain the necessary data exceeds your available resources you should reduce the scope of your inquiry or delay the project until sufficient funding is available. Your statistical analysis, resulting conclusions and actions depend on the quality of your data. More detail on study designs encountered in health care can be found in the text by Rossner (2015). Fowler (2013) provides information on conducting survey research.

Data Preparation and Management

Inevitably, some data processing must be performed regardless of the way in which your data was obtained. In some cases, extensive effort is needed to prepare the data for analysis. It is common to encounter data errors, missing values, and data not in the required format. Project plans frequently underestimate the time and effort required for such data preparation.

Defining data elements and their associated units is a vital part of data preparation. Such documentation is of value to the analyst in reporting results and conducting future investigations along with other analysts who make use of the data in the future. Such definitions are essential in large data collections where data elements are often "encoded," meaning a numeric code is stored instead of a more descriptive entry. This has the advantage of reducing the size of the data repository, minimizing data entry errors, and allows descriptions to be modified over time. Codebooks provide the detailed data definitions. While the use of codes is efficient from a data management perspective, they are not generally meaningful to stakeholders. Therefore, the code descriptions will be needed when preparing reports and visualizations for stakeholders. When collecting your own data, be sure that data definitions and units are documented in the initial data preparation phase. JMP provides features to facilitate documentation such as column notes, value labels, and the ability to store documents and data together in a JMP Project.

JMP provides many features for manipulating data. Table 1.1 on page 5 summarizes some of the commonly used data operations that are illustrated in this casebook. This is by no means an exhaustive list. More detail on data management can be found in the DAMA Guide to the Data Management Body of Knowledge (DAMA International, 2017).

Table 1.1 *Data Operations and JMP Features in this Casebook*

Operation	JMP Feature
Data element definition and documentation	Column Information > Notes
Assessing the extent of missing data	Consumer Research > Categorical > Count Missing Responses
Arithmetic transformations/units conversion	Formula Editor
Assign correct measurement level	Data and Modeling Type
Combine data from two data sets, linking by common data element(s)	Tables > Join
Subsetting data	Rows > Data Filter
Concatenating data elements	Formula Editor function Concat
Create a new variable from existing data elements (derived data)	Formula Editor Cols > Recode

The selection of an appropriate statistical method depends on the measurement levels of the response and predictor variables. Measurement levels are expressed in JMP by defining the modeling and data type for each column. In some circumstances, data elements imported into JMP will not default to the correct data or modeling type. Prior to beginning a JMP analysis check that each data element is assigned the correct data and modeling types.

Another important aspect of data management in health care settings is to protect and control access to data, particularly patient-level data containing personal health information. Organizational data that is propriety, such as personnel and intellectual property information, will also require protection and access controls.

Analysis

Exploring and Summarizing Data

When data preparation is complete, an exploratory data analysis should be undertaken. Familiarity with the data is essential for efficient and informed analysis. A good strategy is to begin with univariate analysis and proceed to bivariate and multivariate exploration. Visualization is the primary tool with support from univariate and bivariate descriptive statistics. For data sets with a large number of variables, automating the exploratory analysis (for example using the JMP Scripting Language) may be necessary.

A thorough exploratory analysis:

▪ Identifies data errors, missing data, outliers, and needed data reformatting,

▪ Familiarizes the analyst with the variation and distribution of each data element,

▪ Suggests relationships between variables that can guide the choice and application of subsequent statistical methods, and

▪ Forms the basis for the key descriptive statistics and visualizations that will be reported to stakeholders.

It is not uncommon to further refine the data set after the initial exploratory analysis to correct data errors, create additional derived data, impute missing data (McKnight et al., 2007), and identify additional data that will be needed.

Table 1.2 on page 7 summarizes some commonly used numerical statistics and the associated JMP platforms that are found in the subsequent cases. Additional explanation of descriptive statistics can be found in Polit (2010) and Rossner (2016).

Table 1.2 *Numerical Statistics and Associated JMP Platforms*

Univariate – Continuous	Univariate – Nominal/Ordinal	Bivariate/Multivariate

• Centrality
  • Mean
  • Median
  • Mode
• Variation
  • Standard deviation
  • Range
  • Interquartile range
  • Minimum and maximum
 	
JMP Platforms:
• *Distribution*
• *Tabulate*
• *Column Viewer*
	• Count and percent in each category
	
	JMP Platforms:
	• *Distribution*
	• *Tabulate*
	• *Column Viewer*
		• Pearson correlation coefficient
		
		JMP Platform:
		• *Multivariate*
		• *Tabulate*

JMP provides many different ways to visualize data. Graph Builder is a very flexible platform for creating simple to complex multivariate visualizations. Other options are available in the Graph menu and in the individual analysis platforms. Table 1.3 on page 7 summarizes those graphs illustrated in this casebook.

Table 1.3 *Data Visualizations Used in This Casebook*

Univariate	Bivariate	Multivariate
• Histogram/Bar Graph • Box plot • Mosaic • Pie chart	• Scatterplot/line graph • Map • Heat map • Mosaic	• Bubble plot • Scatterplot matrix • Map • Tree map

JMP has many features available for enhancing your graphs including annotation, reference lines, and color. Data visualizations are powerful tools for communicating to stakeholders. The reader is referred to the works of Cleveland (1994), Tufte (2001), and Few (2012) for more guidelines on creating compelling data visualizations.

Select and Apply Method

One of the biggest challenges to beginning analysts is to decide which statistical methods to apply to a problem. A good approach is to start with simple analyses such as means comparisons before proceeding to more complex models such as multiple regression analysis. Taking a step-by-step approach allows the analyst to gain insight at each step that guides the next analysis. This yields orderly and efficient problem solving.

Begin by breaking down the problem statement or research question to identify the response of interest, the predictors (if any), and the problem objective. In each case we use three questions to identify an appropriate method to apply:

1   What is the response (Y) of interest and what is its measurement level?

2   Are predictor variables (X) mentioned in the problem statement? If so, how many and what are their measurement levels?

3   What are you being asked to deliver? A data description, an interval estimate, an answer to a question, or a predictive model?

In many cases you must specify the statistical parameter that will be used as the basis for answering your research question. The mean is frequently chosen, but there are circumstances where other measures such as the median, standard deviation, or a selected quantile best address the problem. Table 1.4 on page 8 can assist you in choosing an appropriate analysis method and JMP platform.

Table 1.4   *Guide to Selecting a Statistical Method*

Predictors (X) [Number of predictors]	Response (Y)	
	Nominal/Ordinal	**Continuous**
Univariate [0]	Confidence interval - proportion Test of hypothesis – proportion *JMP Platform: Distribution*	Confidence interval – mean or standard deviation Test of hypothesis - mean or standard deviation *JMP Platform: Distribution*

Predictors (X) [Number of predictors]		Response (Y)	
		Nominal/Ordinal	Continuous
Bivariate [1]	Nominal or Ordinal	Chi-square test for independence or homogeneity *JMP Platform: Fit Y by X*	Paired t-test (Paired samples) *JMP Platform: Distribution or Specialized Modeling > Matched Pairs* Two-independent samples t-test *JMP Platform: Fit Y by X* One-way analysis of variance (more than two samples) *JMP Platform: Fit Y by X*
	Continuous	Logistic regression *JMP Platform: Fit Y by X*	Simple linear regression *JMP Platform: Fit Y by X*
Multivariate [≥2]	Mixed	Multiple logistic regression *JMP Platform: Fit Model* Decision tree *JMP Platform: Partition*	Multiple linear regression *JMP Platform: Fit Model* Decision tree *JMP Platform: Partition*

In addition to identifying the response variable, predictors, and problem objective, knowledge of the study design or data collection method may be needed to choose an appropriate analysis. For example, the appropriate form of the t-test to use when comparing a continuous outcome from two groups depends on whether it is a paired or independent comparison. Assumptions underlying each method should be verified to the extent possible. When assumptions are seriously violated, other methods, such as non-parametric methods, should be pursued. Nonparametric alternatives can generally be found alongside the parametric options, in JMP platforms

Disseminating Results

Interpreting Statistical Results in Context

In health care, the objective of data analysis is to support decisions to improve the quality of patient care, contain costs, and increase efficiency in service delivery. When disseminating statistical results it is not sufficient to simply declare statistical significance (or insignificance). Results must be interpreted in the problem context. For example, a pilot study on the use of fall mats in a memory care facility shows that the number of falls with injury is reduced by an average of one per month with statistical significance. This reduction in fall injuries, while statistically significant, must be evaluated for practical significance by health care professionals. Is the benefit from the reduction in fall injuries cost justified? What are the costs to install, maintain, and clean floor mats? Are there other less expensive alternatives to reducing falls? What risks, such as tripping hazard, are associated with the use of fall mats?

You should think carefully about what your results mean in the problem setting and offer your recommendations to decision makers, within the limitations of your domain knowledge. Your recommendations should be guided by the data and analysis rather than your opinions. You should also offer suggested next actions. Offering solid analysis and impartial recommendations will make you a valuable contributor to the enterprise.

Communicate to Stakeholders

Statistical results, poorly communicated, will not have an impact on the problem or the intended audience. You should craft your communications to meet the needs of your audience in the time or space allowed. Do not try to force 10 minutes of information into a 5 minute presentation. In some cases you will need to prepare different communications for different audiences (e.g., general public, scientific or professional community), taking into consideration their familiarity with the problem domain, terminology, and statistical analysis. For example, in conveying statistical results to the general public it may be sufficient to state that a result is statistically significant, while communicating the same result to a scientific audience may benefit by reporting a p-value.

The following guidelines can assist you in preparing effective data analysis presentations:

- Focus on the problem and how your analysis adds insight.
  - Use the language of the problem domain.
  - Avoid the use of statistical jargon and notation.
  - Organize your information in a way that makes sense to your audience.
- Familiarize your audience with the data.
  - Identify the data source and give data definitions for key variables.

□ Numerical summaries are easily assimilated in tables. Round numbers appropriately and display units.

□ Visualizations allow data distributions, outliers, time trends, and geographic relationships to be easily perceived. Include titles, axis scales and labels. Use color judiciously.

▪ Focus on the essential analytic results as related to the problem

□ Always identify results as being statistically significant or insignificant.

□ State the limitations of the analysis.

□ Identify insights gained from the analysis and the effect of unusual observations.

Your information will be best received if it is focused, concise, relevant, and delivered with enthusiasm.

The twelve cases presented in this book illustrate many of the concepts covered in this introduction. With the exception of one (Visualizing Influenza Activity), the cases focus on six different problems with several cases forming a sequence for each problem. This illustrates a problem-solving approach starting with basic descriptive analysis and building to more complicated statistical inference and modeling. All but one data set were obtained from open sources.

Problems

1 A hospital has established a goal to improve hospital stay conditions and is accepting input from various stakeholders on their ideal vision of "What is a good hospital stay?"

a Adopt a perspective, for example, a patient, a clinician, an administrator, and refine the question to one that can be answered using data.

b Identify variables that can be collected to address the research question. For each variable state its measurement level and JMP modeling type.

2 Search the Internet for data sources on mortality from firearms. Discuss potential biases that may be present from each data source. Which data source would you recommend using and why?

3 Develop a research question on a topic of your choice.

a Find a data source that has an accompanying codebook.

b Identify the data elements that correspond to the response and predictors of your research question.

   c Critically evaluate the codebook and any other associated documents. Are the data definitions clear and complete? Is there sufficient background information to understand the data's pedigree?

   d Conduct a basic descriptive analysis of your chosen variables using both visualizations and descriptive statistics.

4 Create a JMP data table that has one column named "Zip Code." Enter the zip code 02135 (Boston, MA).

   a What is the correct measurement level for a zip code?

   b Change the JMP data and modeling types and notice the effect. What are the correct JMP data and modeling types for a zip code?

   c What are the consequences of using an incorrect data or modeling type in a statistical analysis or when visualizing data?

5 Search the print and digital media to find examples of effective and ineffective data presentation. For each example identify the following.

   a Who is the intended audience?

   b What about the data presentation effectively communicates to the audience?

   c What about the data presentation could be improved?

References

Cleveland, William S., *The Elements of Graphing Data*, 2nd ed., Hobart Press, 1994.

DAMA International, *DAMA Guide to the Data Management Body of Knowledge*, 2nd ed., Technics Press, 2017.

Few, Stephen, *Show Me the Numbers: Designing Tables and Graphs to Enlighten*, 2nd ed., Analytics Press, 2012.

Fowler, F. J., Jr., *Survey Research Methods*, 5th ed., Sage Publications, 2013.

McKnight, P.E., K. M. McKnight, S. Sidani, and A. J. Figueredo, *Missing Data: A Gentle Introduction*, Guildford Press, 2007.

Polit, D. F., *Statistics and Data Analysis for Nursing Research*, 2nd ed., Pearson, 2010.

Rossner, B., *Fundamentals of Biostatistics*, 8th ed., Cengage Learning, 2015.

Tufte, Edward R., *The Visual Display of Quantitative Information*, 2nd ed., Graphics Press, 2001.

2

Nurses' Perceptions of Evidence-based Practice: Assessing the Current Culture

Chapter Summary Concepts

Statistical Concepts	Data Management Concepts	JMP Features
Descriptive statistics	Treatment of missing data	Distribution
Data visualization • Histogram • Mosaic plot	Data preparation	List Check
Confidence interval for a proportion	Recoding	Data Filter
		Excluding Rows
		Tablulate

Background

A "magnet" hospital is one that has been recognized by the American Nurses Credentialing Center for nursing excellence. Patients can expect to receive high quality care at magnet organizations. Nurses at magnet hospitals report higher levels of job satisfaction compared to those that do not have the magnet designation. Hospitals benefit from improved patient outcomes and the ability to attract and retain high quality nursing staff. Achieving magnet designation is a rigorous process that requires hospitals to demonstrate excellence in five areas, one of which is evidence-based practice (EBP). EBP is an approach to nursing that integrates nursing research, a nurse's clinical experience and skill, and patient values when making patient care decisions.

A 450-bed hospital is pursuing magnet designation. To assess the extent to which EBP is integrated into its culture, the Nursing Research and Evidence-based Practice Council conducted a survey of the hospital's registered nurses. The survey (Gale and Schaffer, 2009) was designed to answer a number of questions related to evidence-based practice and the state of the hospital's nursing culture.

Problem Statement

Initially, the Nursing Research and Evidence-based Practice Council wanted to know if registered nurses viewed the hospital's EBP changes positively. This is best represented by the response to the survey question "All of the practice changes so far have been practical and fit well with the workflow of the unit." This is one of seven statements about evidence-based practice where the nurses were asked to rate the hospital's performance.

The Data

The online survey was offered to all registered nurses employed by the hospital. A total of 854 nurses were invited to take the survey. Upon opening the survey, the respondent was asked to give their consent to participate in the survey. If consent was not given, the survey application closed.

The data from selected survey questions and respondent demographics is contained in the file EBP_Survey_Responses.jmp and data definitions are given at the end of this case. A copy of the complete survey can be found in the online resources that accompany this book.

Data Management

Checking for Data Anomalies

Prior to conducting analysis, the data should be examined for anomalies. A good first step is to review the histograms for each column. Select Analyze > Distribution and enter all of the columns into the Y Columns field.

Figure 2.1 on page 16 shows the histogram for the column Primary Role, which reveals that three Licensed Practical Nurses (LPN) responded to the survey.

Figure 2.1 *Histogram for Primary Role*

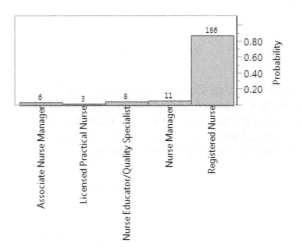

Only registered nurses were eligible to take the survey, therefore the LPN responses should not be included in the analysis. Associate nurse managers, nurse educators/quality specialists, and nurse managers are required to be registered nurses. The rows containing the LPN responses can be found using Row > Data Filter, as shown in Figure 2.2 on page 16.

Figure 2.2 *Data Filter to Select LPN Responses*

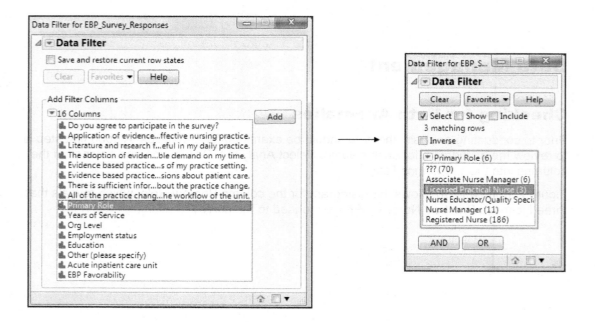

The data table will have three rows highlighted. Right-click one of the highlighted rows and select the Exclude/Unexclude toggle. Excluding a row will omit that observation from calculations, but it will be shown on JMP graphs. Observations can be omitted from graphs using the Hide/Unhide toggle. An observation can be both excluded and hidden with the Exclude and Hide toggle. The presence of three ineligible survey responses warrants investigation into the survey design and distribution process.

Figure 2.3 on page 17 shows the histogram for Primary Role for the eligible survey respondents.

Figure 2.3   *Histogram for Primary Role (2)*

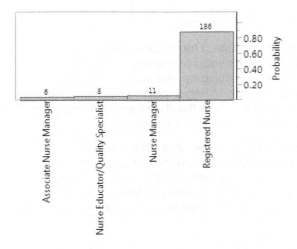

Calculating Survey Response Rate

It is important to give the response rate when presenting survey results. The Distribution output for the consent question, "Do you agree to participate in the survey?" is shown in Figure 2.4 on page 18.

Figure 2.4 *Distribution for Survey Consent*

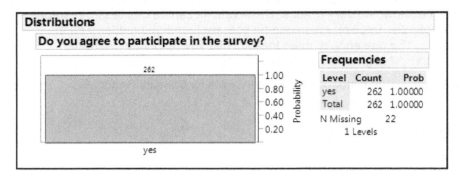

There are 262 affirmative responses and 22 missing values. The missing values exist because of the way in which the survey tool operates. As soon as the application is opened a record is created. If a respondent does not consent to participate, the survey application closes without recording a value in the "Consent" column. When importing data into JMP that is created by other software, it is important to understand how the data records are created. For this survey, 22 respondents who opened the survey tool did not consent.

Taking into account the three ineligible LPN responses and the 22 nurses who did not consent to the survey there are a total of 259 valid responses and the correct response rate is 259/854 = 30%. It will be easier to find the non-response rates for the various survey questions to create a new data table that contains only the valid survey responses. This can be done by selecting the rows corresponding to the valid responses and creating a new table using Tables > Subset.

Analytic Approach

The three questions below will guide the selection of appropriate methods to address the following research question:

How did the nurses respond to the survey question, "All of the practice changes so far have been practical and fit well with the workflow of the unit"?

1 What is the response (Y) of interest and how is it measured? The response of interest is the nurses' opinion of the current state of EBP at the hospital as measured by the rating question "All of the practice changes so far have been practical and fit well with the workflow of the unit." There are five response options for this question expressing the degree of agreement with the statement. This is an example of a 5-point Likert scale. The Likert scale is often used in surveys to measure attitudes and opinions and is an ordinal scale of measure. Ordinal data has an implied ordering or ranking and is summarized as the proportion of responses in each of the five rating categories.

2 Are predictor variables (X) mentioned in the problem statement? If so, how many and what are their measurement levels? The problem statement does not ask about predictors of attitude toward EBP.

3 What are you being asked to deliver? A data description, an interval estimate, an answer to a question, or a predictive model? An estimate of the proportion of nurses that view the current state of EBP favorably will address the problem statement. Since this is a sample statistic and subject to sampling error, a confidence interval will provide a range of plausible values for the true proportion of nurses that view EBP favorably.

JMP Analysis

Descriptive Analysis

You should begin with a descriptive analysis for the survey rating question "All of the practice changes so far have been practical and fit well with the workflow of the unit." This can be done with the Distribution platform. The JMP output is shown in Figure 2.5 on page 19.

Figure 2.5 *JMP Distribution Output for Response to the Survey Question "All of the practice changes so far have been practical and fit well with the workflow of the unit"*

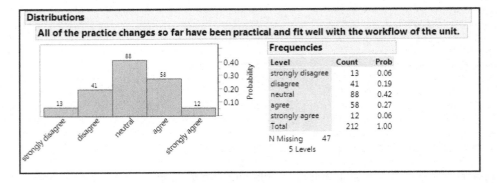

To round the proportion in each category, right click any of the values in the Prob column, select Format Column and choose the appropriate number of decimal places.

Notice that 47 (18%) of the nurses chose not to give a rating. The proportions given in the Frequency table are based on the number of nurses who responded to this particular question.

Neutral is the most frequently occurring response with 42% of the nurses selecting this rating. The histogram and the frequency table present the same information. When reporting these results, choose the presentation format that will be most easily understood by your audience.

A descriptive analysis of the respondents' demographics will provide additional insight into the survey results. A table of descriptive statistics can be created with the JMP Tabulate platform (Analyze > Tabulate). Highlight the four columns containing the demographic variables (Primary Role, Years of Service, Employment Status, and Education) and drag them to the drop zone for rows, then highlight N and % of Total from the column of statistics and drag them to the drop zone for columns. Adjust the format so the % of Total is rounded as shown in Figure 2.6 on page 20.

Figure 2.6 *Tabulate Dialog to Create Table of Nurse Demographics*

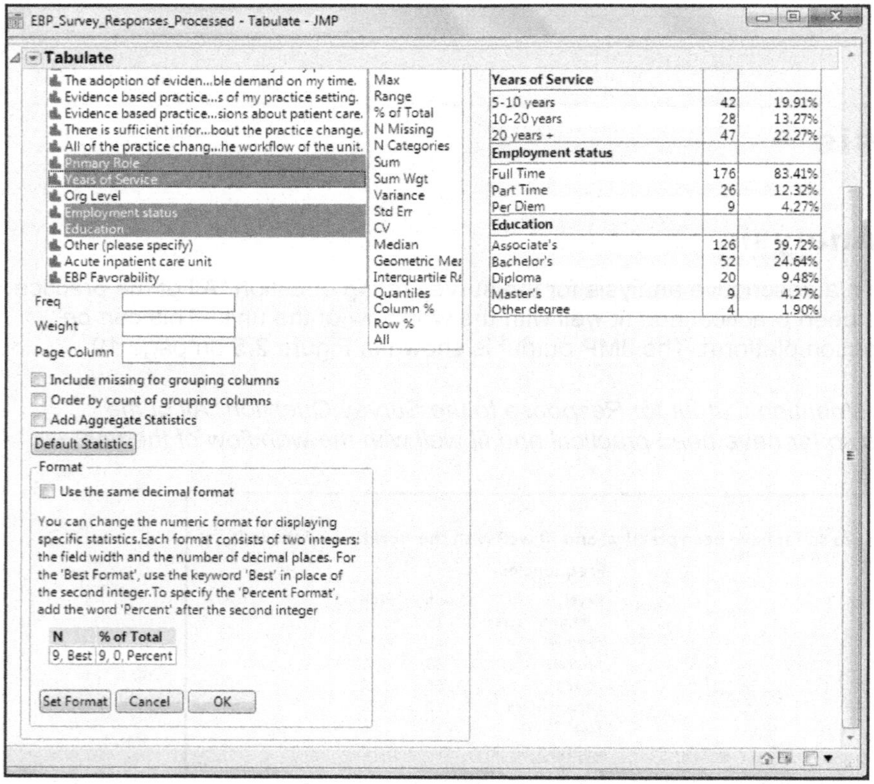

Figure 2.7 on page 21 shows the resulting table containing the frequency distributions for each of the demographic variables.

Figure 2.7 *JMP Tabulate Output for Nurse Demographics*

Tabulate

Primary Role	N	% of Total
Associate Nurse Manager	6	3%
Nurse Educator/Quality Specialist	8	4%
Nurse Manager	11	5%
Registered Nurse	186	88%
Years of Service		
Less than one year	20	9%
1-3 years	42	20%
3-5 years	32	15%
5-10 years	42	20%
10-20 years	28	13%
20 years +	47	22%
Employment status		
Full Time	176	83%
Part Time	26	12%
Per Diem	9	4%
Education		
Associate's	126	60%
Bachelor's	52	25%
Diploma	20	9%
Master's	9	4%
Other degree	4	2%

We see that 88% of the nurses are registered nurses, there is a fairly uniform distribution of years of service with the hospital, 83% of the nurses are employed full time, and 60% hold an associate's degree. A descriptive analysis is a necessary first step in your data analysis. It is important to give your audience a statistical summary of the data you have collected.

Confidence Interval for the Proportion of Nurses Who View EBP Favorably

The proportion of nurses that view the current state of EBP favorably would correspond to responses for the agree and strongly agree ratings. The neutral, disagree, and strongly disagree ratings can be combined to indicate those nurses that do not rate EBP favorably. Create a new column, "EBP Favorability" that combines the agree and strongly agree responses into a "Favorable" level and the remaining responses combine into the "Not Favorable" level. This new column can be created using the JMP recoding feature. Before using the Recode command, you will need to remove the List Check option from the column containing the responses to this survey question. For this recoding, we want to create a new column called "EBP Favorability" by highlighting the column "All of the practice changes so far have been practical and fit well with the workflow of the unit" and selecting Cols > Recode and choosing "New Column" option, as shown in Figure 2.8 on page 22.

Figure 2.8 *Completed Recode Dialog to Create EBP Favorability Column*

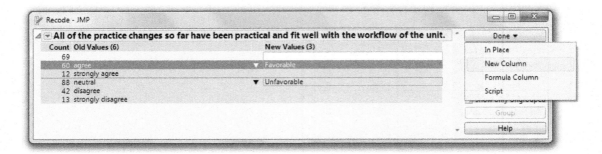

We do not want to overwrite the original 5-point Likert responses as they may be needed in a future analysis.

The JMP Distribution platform allows us to summarize the EBP Favorability column and compute a confidence interval for the proportion of nurses who view EBP favorably. The frequency distribution for the EBP Favorability column is shown in tabular and graphical form in Figure 2.9 on page 22. The mosaic plot was obtained from the red triangle menu.

Figure 2.9 *JMP Distribution Output for EBP Favorability*

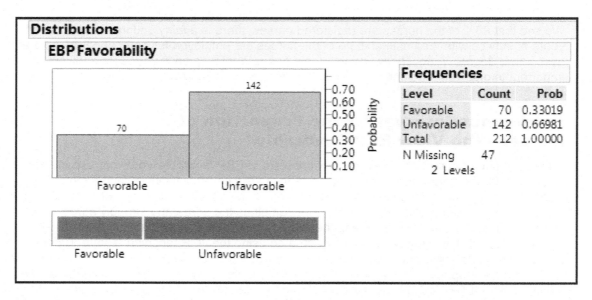

The histogram shows more detailed information than does the mosaic plot. The mosaic plot may be a preferable visualization when there are space limitations or a large number of nominal or ordinal variables to summarize. Of the nurses that responded to the survey, 33% have a favorable opinion of the current implementation of EBP changes in their unit.

A confidence interval for the proportion of nurses who view EBP favorably can be obtained from the Distribution platform by selecting Confidence Interval from the red triangle menu associated with the EBP Favorability variable. A 95% confidence level is chosen for this case. Figure 2.10 on page 23 shows the JMP confidence interval output.

Figure 2.10 *JMP Confidence Interval Output for EBP Favorability*

EBP Favorability					
Confidence Intervals					
Level	Count	Prob	Lower CI	Upper CI	1-Alpha
Favorable	70	0.33	0.27	0.40	0.95
Unfavorable	142	0.67	0.60	0.73	0.95
Total	212				
Note: Computed using score confidence intervals.					

The best estimate of the proportion of nurses that view EBP favorably is 0.33. A 95% confidence interval for the proportion of respondents who view the EBP implementation favorably is [0.27, 0.40]. There is 95% confidence that the true proportion of respondents who view EBP changes at the hospital favorably lies between 0.27 and 0.40. The 95% confidence level means that on repeated sampling we would expect 95% of such intervals to contain the true proportion. Different confidence levels can be chosen, but 95% is commonly used in health care applications. The confidence interval takes into account the precision with which the sample proportion was estimated.

Analysis Implications

Analysis of the question that seeks to assess the opinion of the current state of EBP shows that only 33% of the nurses viewed EBP favorably. A 95% confidence interval of [0.27, 0.40] is a range of plausible values for the true proportion favoring EBP and accounts for the uncertainty associated with estimating the sample proportion.

The survey represents the opinions of a minority of the nurses at the hospital since the response rate was 30%. This survey was voluntary and as such the data constitute a non-random sample. Random sampling is an assumption that underlies the confidence interval method. Surveys such as this are subject to self-selection bias. Nurses who chose to respond to the survey may have been more interested in EBP or hold stronger opinions about the success of EBP to date. This means that the results may not be representative of the population of registered nurses. Conclusions drawn must be tempered by the 30% response rate, non-random sampling and the potential self-selection bias.

The confidence interval gives the Nursing Research and Evidence-based Practice Council an initial understanding of the perception of EBP among the registered nurses. Such a preliminary assessment can help them begin to consider ways in which the perception of EBP can be improved. This may include developing training and mentoring programs or revising work practices. Analysis of the other survey questions will provide a more complete understanding of the nurses' opinion of the EBP implementation. As a next step, it would be important to understand if the perception of EBP differs based on demographic factors such as a nurse's organizational level or educational level. As the survey analysis progresses, missing data pattern analysis should be conducted to gain insight into survey nonresponse.

Data Definitions

Primary Role	Job title: nurse manager/associate nurse manager/ nurse educator or quality specialist/registered nurse
Years of Service	Number of years employed as a nurse at this hospital
Org Level	Organizational level is either Leader or Nurse Professional
Employment status	Full-time/part-time/per diem
Education	Highest nursing degree held
Acute inpatient care unit	Hospital unit where the nurse works
EBP Favorability	Aggregation of responses to the question "All of the practice changes so far have been practical and fit well with the workflow of the unit." Favorable contains the agree and strongly agree responses, Unfavorable contains strongly disagree, disagree and neutral
Practicality & Workflow 3 point	Aggregation of responses to the question "Evidence based practice does not take into account the limitations of my practice setting." Agreement contains the agree and strongly agree responses, Disagreement contains strongly disagree, disagree and neutral

Problems

1 Use Graph > Chart to create visualizations of the variables "All of the practice changes so far have been practical and fit well with the workflow of the unit" and "EBP Favorability" different from those presented in this case. Which of these visualizations would you recommend and why?

2 Repeat the analysis presented in this case for the survey question "The adoption of evidence based practice puts an unreasonable demand on my time." How do the nurses' opinion on this question compare with those of the question "All of the practice changes so far have been practical and fit well with the workflow of the unit."

3 Select another survey question of your choice and conduct an analysis similar to what was done in this case. Prepare a presentation slide that summarizes your analysis.

4 Research and discuss actions that can be taken when designing and executing a survey to maximize survey response. How could these actions have been applied in this case?

References

Stevens, Kathleen R., "The Impact of Evidence-Based Practice in Nursing and the Next Big Ideas," The Online Journal of Issues in Nursing, Vol. 18, No.2, May 2013, accessed on November 9, 2015 at http://nursingworld.org/MainMenuCategories/ANAMarketplace/ANAPeriodicals/OJIN/TableofContents/Vol-18-2013/No2-May-2013/Impact-of-Evidence-Based-Practice.html?css=print.

Gale BVP and Schaffer MA, "Organizational readiness for evidence-based practice," Journal of Nursing Administration, 2009; 39(2):91-97.

3

Nurses' Perceptions of Evidence-based Practice: Does It Differ by Organization Level?

Chapter Summary Concepts

Statistical Concepts	Data Management Concepts	JMP Features
Descriptive statistics	Treatment of missing data	Fit Y by X
Data visualization • Mosaic plot	Aggregating variables	Recode
X^2 test of independence		Categorical
Validating assumptions		Tabulate

Background

This is the second case examining the results of a survey that assesses the state of evidence-based practice (EBP) at a 450-bed hospital that is pursuing magnet designation. Hospitals are recognized with magnet designation after successfully completing a rigorous process to demonstrate nursing excellence. Evidence-based practice is one component of nursing excellence and integrates nursing research, a nurse's clinical experience and skill, and patient values when providing patient care. Magnet hospitals benefit from improved patient outcomes and the ability to attract and retain high quality nursing staff.

To assess the nursing culture and the extent to which EBP is integrated into its culture, the Nursing Research and Evidence-based Practice Council sponsored a survey (Gale and Schaffer, 2009) which was offered to all of the hospital's registered nurses. Registered nurses fall into one of two categories, nurse leaders and nurse professionals. Nurse leaders include nurse managers, associate nurse managers, and nurse educators/quality specialists and are primarily responsible for supervision and education. Registered nurses, whose main responsibilities are to deliver direct patient care, are referred to as nurse professionals.

In the first case in this series, we prepared the data and analyzed one of the survey questions to provide an overall assessment of the nurses' opinions of EBP as implemented at the hospital. The important findings from that case were that the proportion of nurses that viewed EBP favorably is 0.33. A 95% confidence interval for the proportion is [0.27, 0.40] and accounts for the uncertainty associated with estimating the sample proportion.

In this case we will gain a deeper understanding of the nurses' perception of the implementation of EBP in their units. We will analyze their perceptions of EBP as related to both the workflow in their units and their practice setting. Examples of practice settings include emergency departments, operating rooms, or intensive care units. In addition, we will compare perceptions based on organization level (nurse leaders or nurse professionals).

Problem Statement

The Nursing Research and Evidence-based Practice Council would like to know if there are differences in how the leaders and nurse professionals view EBP changes with respect to the working environment, particularly unit workflow and practice setting.

The Data

The problem statement can be addressed by analyzing two of the seven survey questions that ask the nurses to rate the implementation of EBP in their hospital unit:

- "All of the practice changes so far have been practical and fit well with the workflow of the unit."
- "Evidence based practice does not take into account the limitations of my practice setting."

The online survey was offered to all registered nurses employed by the hospital. A total of 854 nurses were invited to participate. The survey includes seven rating questions that pertain to excellence in EBP. The nurses were asked to rate each of these questions on a five-point Likert scale. The responses for these seven questions and participant demographics are contained in the file EBP_Survey_Responses2.jmp. Data definitions are given at the end of this case. A copy of the complete survey can be found in the online resources that accompany this book.

Data Management

Creating a Column for Organizational Level

The problem statement is looking for differences in perception by organizational level, specifically between the nurse leaders and nurse professionals. The survey did not collect this information directly, but rather requested the respondent's specific job title. To address the problem statement a new variable must be created that maps the various job titles into the two organizational categories. Highlight the column Primary Role and then select Cols > Utilities > Recode. Assign the nurse manager, associate nurse manager, and nurse educator/quality specialist the level "leader" and the registered nurse the level "nurse professional." Create a new column entitled "Org Level" by selecting "New Column" from the Done drop-down menu.

The JMP Categorical platform can be used to create a table showing the number of responses and associated percentages in each of the two organizational levels. From the Analyze menu, select Consumer Research > Categorical with the "Count Missing Responses" option chosen as shown in Figure 3.1 on page 30.

Figure 3.1 *Completed Categorical Dialog to Obtain Distribution of Organization Level*

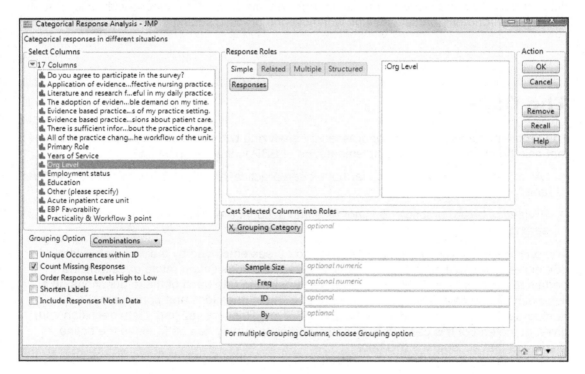

The resulting table is shown in Figure 3.2 on page 31.

Figure 3.2 on page 31 shows the distribution of nurse leaders and nurse professionals who responded to the survey which was obtained from Analyze > Consumer Research > Categorical with the "Count Missing Responses" option selected.

Figure 3.2 *Distribution of Org Level*

Responses(Org Level)			
Freq	Org Level		
Share	Leader	Nurse Professional	Total Responses
All	48	25	186	259
	18.5%	9.7%	71.8%	

Forty-eight (18.5%) nurses chose not to give their job title.

Calculating Survey Response Rate by Organizational Level

Examining non-response can provide valuable insights when interpreting survey results. Of the 259 nurses responding to the survey, 25 (10%) were leaders and 186 (72%) were nurse professionals. Table 3.1 on page 31 compares the response frequencies by organization level to the frequencies found in the hospital's nursing population.

Table 3.1 *Non-response Analysis*

Organization Level	Response Frequency (%)	Population Frequency (%)
Nurse Professional	186 (88)	811 (95)
Leader	25 (12)	43 (5)

The leaders responded to the survey in greater proportion than did the nurse professionals in comparison to their occurrence in the hospital's nursing population. This means that the opinions of the leaders are overrepresented in the survey.

Analytic Approach

In this case we are want to determine if there are differences in how the leaders and nurse professionals view EPB changes in their unit workflow and practice setting. The three questions below will guide the selection of appropriate statistical methods.

1 What is the response (Y) of interest and how is it measured? Two of the survey's rating questions are being analyzed in this case. There are five response options for each of these questions expressing the degree of agreement with each proposition. This is referred to as a 5-point Likert scale and is an ordinal scale of measure. Since this is an ordinal scale, we are interested in the frequency (or proportion) of response in each of the five agreement categories.

2 Are predictor variables mentioned in the problem statement? If so, how many and what are their measurement levels? The problem statement concerns differences in the perception of EBP by organization level. In this case we are interested in comparing the opinions of leaders vs. nurse professionals. This means there is one predictor variable (X), the organization level.

3 What are you being asked to deliver? A data description, an interval estimate, an answer to a question, or a predictive model? We are being asked to answer a question. A test of hypothesis is an appropriate statistical method to answer a question based on a sample of data. For this case we will make two bivariate comparisons, where the response variable (Y) is the rating and the predictor variable (X) is the organization level. The appropriate statistical method is a chi-square test for independence.

Chi-Square Test for Independence

We want to know if a nurse's perception of EBP depends on their organizational level. A chi-square test is the appropriate method for comparing two nominal or ordinal variables. The null hypothesis for this test is that perception is independent of organization level. The alternative hypothesis is that perception depends on organization level.

If the null hypothesis is true, that there is no difference in perception by organization level, then we would expect to see the same proportion in each rating category for both the nurse professionals and the nurse leaders. If the proportions are not close between the nurse professionals and the nurse leaders, we would suspect that their perceptions of EBP differ. As with other hypothesis tests, we need to ascertain that the differences we see are statistically significant and not due to sampling error. We will use a chi-square test statistic. This measures the discrepancy between the frequencies we observed in our sample and what we would expect under the null hypothesis. The chi-square test statistic follows a chi-square distribution.

When comparing two nominal/ordinal variables, it is customary to present the data in a contingency table. In our case, we have two organization levels and five response levels, so our contingency table will have two rows and five columns. Each "cell" of the table contains the frequency for each combination of organization and response level. An important assumption in conducting a chi-square test for independence is that no more than 20% of the cells can have expected frequencies of five or less. We also assume that the survey responses are independent. The chi-square test concerns the independence of the two factors – organization level and perception. The assumption of independence has to do with how the data was collected, i.e., a participant's response is not influenced or related to the response of another participant.

JMP Analysis

Descriptive Analysis

Every analysis should begin by describing and graphing the data. In the case "Nurses' Perception of Evidence-based Practice: Assessing the Current Culture" the demographic characteristics for all nurses were summarized with descriptive statistics as shown in Figure 1.5. Since we are interested in differences by organizational level we will summarize the nurses' demographic characteristics by organizational level using Tabulate. Drag and drop the demographic characteristics into the drop zone for rows and then drag and drop N and Column % into the drop zone for columns. Now drag Org level to the top of the N and Column % cells. The complete table is shown in Figure 3.3 on page 34.

When expressing percentages in a table, there are three choices for how the percentage can be calculated: as a percent of total number of observations, as a percent of the column totals, or as a percent of the row totals. The choice of which percentage to display depends on the analysis objective. In this case we are interested in comparing by organizational level and since that is the column variable in the table, column % is selected. Comparing the demographic characteristics between nurse professionals and leaders we see that:

- Leaders have one of three different primary roles, while nurse professionals have only one primary role.

- Leaders tend to have more years of service than nurse professionals.

- Leaders are all full-time employees, while most nurse professionals are full-time with 19% having part-time employment status.

- Leaders tend to have higher education levels than nurse professionals.

Understanding the demographic differences between the two groups of nurses is valuable when interpreting the differences in their perceptions of EBP.

Figure 3.3 *JMP Tabulate Output for Nurse Demographics by Organizational Level*

Tabulate

| | | Org Level | | |
| | | Leader | | Nurse Professional |
Primary Role	N	Column %	N	Column %
Associate Nurse Manager	6	24%	0	0%
Nurse Educator/Quality Specialist	8	32%	0	0%
Nurse Manager	11	44%	0	0%
Registered Nurse	0	0%	186	100%
Years of Service				
Less than one year	0	0%	20	11%
1-3 years	1	4%	41	22%
3-5 years	5	20%	27	15%
5-10 years	9	36%	33	18%
10-20 years	4	16%	24	13%
20 years +	6	24%	41	22%
Employment status				
Full Time	25	100%	151	81%
Part Time	0	0%	26	14%
Per Diem	0	0%	9	5%
Education				
Associate's	11	44%	115	62%
Bachelor's	7	28%	45	24%
Diploma	2	8%	18	10%
Master's	3	12%	6	3%
Other degree	2	8%	2	1%

We will summarize the responses to the two survey questions of interest first overall and then by organization level using Analyze > Consumer Research > Categorical. Select Simple for the Response Roles and check the box for Count Missing Responses.

Figure 3.4 on page 35 shows the completed Categorical dialog.

Figure 3.4 *Completed Categorical Dialog for Survey Question "All of the practice changes so far have been practical and fit well with the workflow of the unit"*

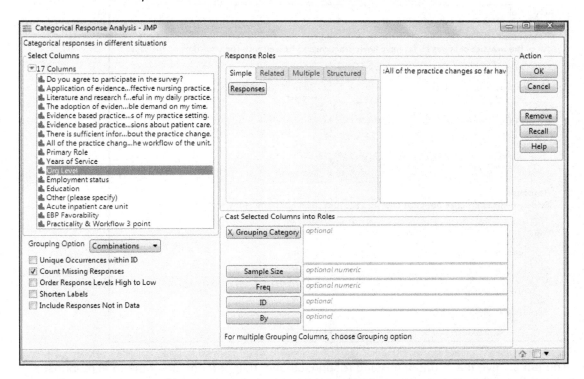

Figure 3.5 on page 36 shows a descriptive analysis for all respondents combined for the two survey questions "All of the practice changes so far have been practical and fit well with the workflow of the unit" and "Evidence based practice does not take into account the limitations of my practice setting" in both tabular and graphical form.

Figure 3.5 *Categorical Response Analysis of Two Survey Questions*

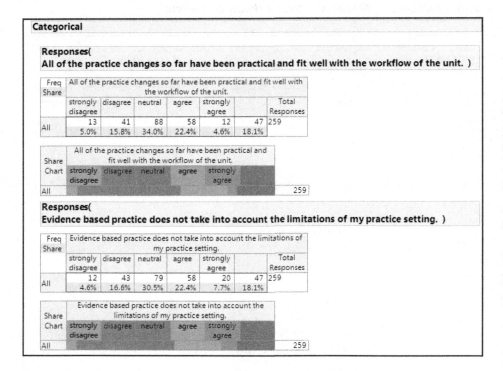

The tables give the count of missing responses and their percentage of the total responses. Alternatively, the missing values can be omitted by leaving "Count Missing Responses" unchecked in the Categorical dialog.

Both questions show a similar pattern of agreement and have the same number of nurses who did not offer a rating. Notice that the question about unit workflow is phrased positively and the question about practice setting is phrased in the negative. In general, the nurses are more positive about EBP with respect to practicality and workflow but view EBP more negatively in terms of practice setting. Best practice in survey design favors phrasing all questions positively. Mixing questions that are phrased both positively and negatively can be confusing to the respondent and may lead to unintended response choices.

Figure 3.6 on page 37 shows survey responses to the two questions by organization level. Again, you can obtain this output by selecting Analyze>Consumer Research>Categorical and enter the column Org Level into the X grouping category.

Figure 3.6 *Categorical Response Analysis of Two Survey Questions by Organizational Level*

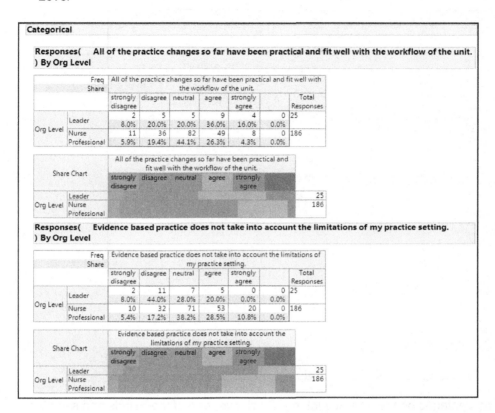

For the rating question on EBP practicality and workflow the nurse professionals had a higher level of neutral response than did the leaders who generally are in more agreement with the proposition. The leaders generally felt that EBP took practice settings limitations into account while nurse professionals did not. Descriptive analysis allows you to observe differences between the organizational levels but does not tell you if these differences are statistically significant. A test of hypothesis is needed to determine statistically significant differences.

Chi-square Test for Independence

Fit Y by X is the appropriate platform to conduct a chi-square test for independence. For this analysis, the column containing the responses to a survey question is the Y and the variable Org Level is the X, as shown in Figure 3.7 on page 38.

Figure 3.7 *Completed Fit Y by X Dialog.*

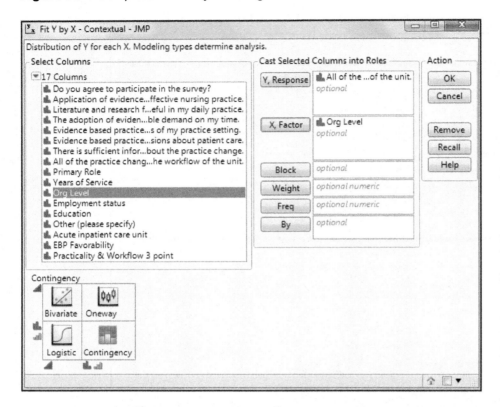

To show the percentages on the mosaic plot, right click over one of the panels and select Cell Labeling > Show Percents. Figure 3.8 on page 39 shows the JMP output for the practicality and workflow question.

Figure 3.8   *Chi-square Analysis for the Practicality and Workflow Question*

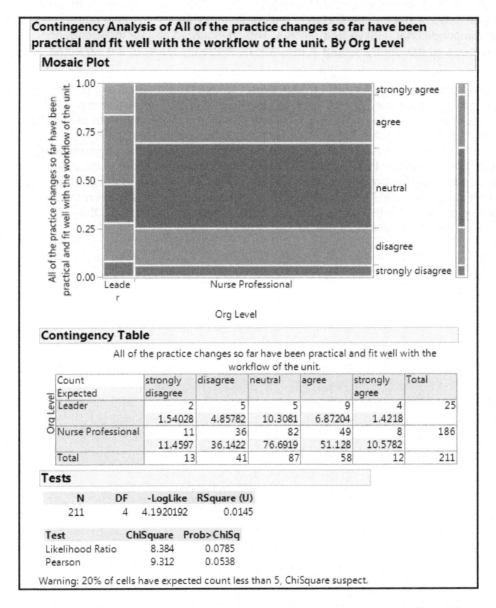

The large mosaic plot shows the proportion of responses in each rating category by each of the organization levels. The small mosaic plot to the right shows the proportion of responses in each rating category for both nurse professionals and leaders combined. This represents the null hypothesis of independence, i.e., both organization levels have the same proportion in each rating category. If the mosaic plots by organization level are similar, then this is consistent with the null hypothesis of independence. Less similarity between the mosaic plots for the two organization levels suggests the data is not consistent with the null hypothesis.

The contingency table displays the observed counts and the counts that would be expected if the pattern of agreement is independent of the organization level. The red triangle menu offers a variety of options that can be shown in the contingency table, including both conditional and unconditional relative frequencies. The chi-squared test for independence compares the observed frequency (Count in the JMP contingency table) to the expected frequency.

We can't establish statistical significance through visual comparison of graphs or comparing the counts in a contingency table. The chi-square test statistic and the associated p-value (Prob>ChiSq) are found in the Tests section. However, the warning at the bottom of the JMP output indicates that the chi-square assumption for the minimum number of cells with expected counts greater than 5 is not satisfied. You can remedy this problem by combining some of the response columns. In this case we can reduce the 5-point Likert scale to a 3-point scale by combining the strongly disagree and disagree categories and the strongly agree and agree categories. JMP's Recode feature provides an easy means to create a column containing the levels disagreement, neutral, and agreement. Rerunning the chi-square analysis yields the results in Figure 3.9 on page 41 .

Figure 3.9 *Chi-square Analysis for the Practicality and Workflow Question with a 3-point Scale*

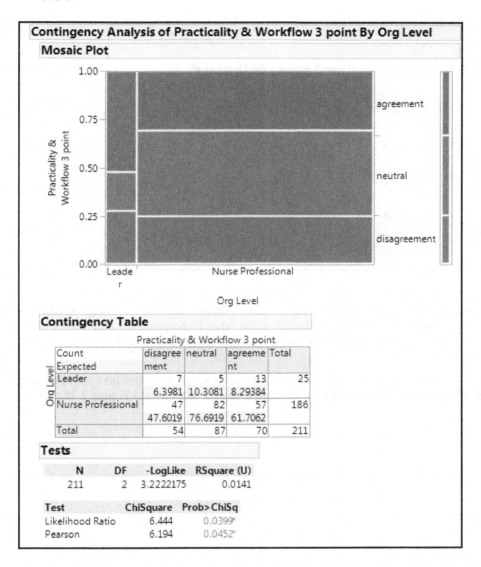

Contingency Analysis of Practicality & Workflow 3 point By Org Level

Mosaic Plot

Contingency Table

Practicality & Workflow 3 point

Count Expected	disagree ment	neutral	agreeme nt	Total
Leader	7	5	13	25
	6.3981	10.3081	8.29384	
Nurse Professional	47	82	57	186
	47.6019	76.6919	61.7062	
Total	54	87	70	211

Tests

N	DF	-LogLike	RSquare (U)
211	2	3.2222175	0.0141

Test	ChiSquare	Prob>ChiSq
Likelihood Ratio	6.444	0.0399*
Pearson	6.194	0.0452*

Note that the chi-square assumption is now satisfied and we can safely use the p-value from the Pearson chi-square test (0.0452) which tells us that at the 5% significance level the perception of EBP with respect to practicality and workflow depends on whether you are a leader or a nurse professional. P-values that are less than the chosen significance level cause a rejection of the null hypothesis. A p-value is the likelihood of obtaining the sample outcome, or something more extreme, assuming the null hypothesis is true. Figure 3.10 on page 42 shows the distribution of the response for the two organization levels.

Figure 3.10   *Categorical Response Analysis of the Practicality and Workflow Question by Organizational Level*

Categorical

Responses(Practicality & Workflow 3 point) By Org Level

Freq Share		Practicality & Workflow 3 point			
		disagreement	neutral	agreement	Total Responses
Org Level	Leader	7	5	13	25
		28.0%	20.0%	52.0%	
	Nurse Professional	47	82	57	186
		25.3%	44.1%	30.6%	

Share Chart		Practicality & Workflow 3 point		
		disagreement	neutral	agreement
Org Level	Leader			25
	Nurse Professional			186

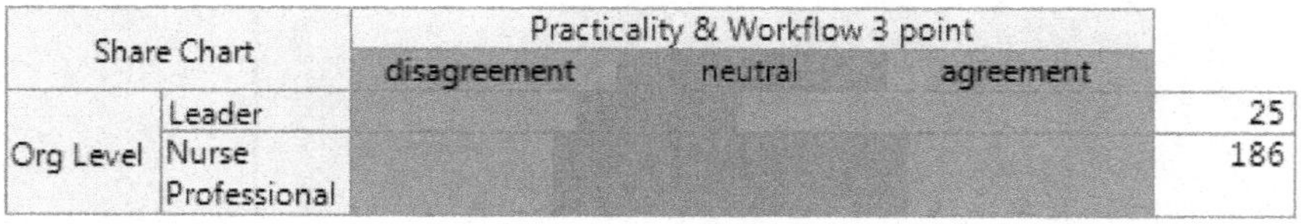

The leaders show a slight majority in agreement while the nurse professionals most frequently respond with neutral and have slightly more in agreement than in disagreement. So for the proposition "All of the practice changes so far have been practical and fit well with the workflow of the unit," the nurse professionals and nurse leaders differ in their patterns of agreement.

Finally, we consider the survey question "Evidence based practice does not take into account the limitations of my practice setting." The chi-square analysis is shown in Figure 3.11 on page 43.

Figure 3.11 *Chi-square Analysis for the Limitations of Practice Setting Question*

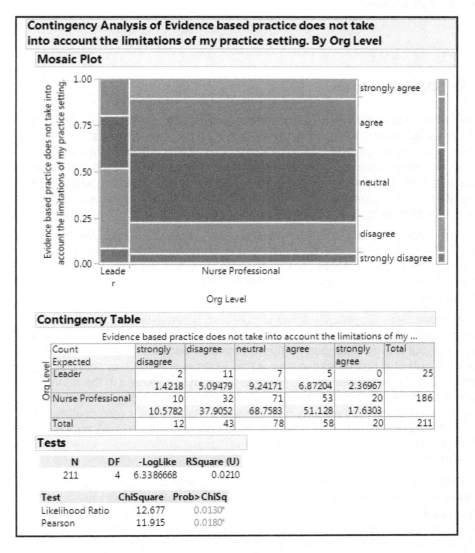

For this survey question, the chi-square assumption for the minimum number of cells with counts of at least five is satisfied and the p-value of 0.0180 from the Pearson test indicates that there is a statistically significant difference at the 5% level in how leaders and nurse professionals view EBP in relation to the limitations of their practice setting. Figure 3.5 on page 36 shows the differences in the support for the proposition with leaders generally finding EBP is consistent with practice setting limitations while the nurse professionals do not.

Finally, we address the assumption of independence between survey respondents. This assumption is best satisfied during the design and administration of the survey. For example, sending the survey link to a respondent's home email rather than their work email may reduce the influence of co-workers.

Analysis Implications

The analysis of two of the seven survey questions shows statistically significant differences in perception between leaders and nurse professionals. Based on these findings, the Nursing Research and Evidence-based Practice Council Analysis can take a number of actions to continue to refine their understanding of the barriers and facilitators to EBP. This can be done by continuing to analyze the survey results and further investigating the ways in which EBP has been implemented at the hospital. For example, have leaders received more training in EBP or do their work responsibilities allow them more time to engage in nursing research?

Our analysis showed a significant difference in how the different organization levels perceive EBP in the context of the practice setting, so a next logical step would be to examine the responses by the variable "Acute inpatient care unit" which identifies the care setting (e.g., intensive care, labor and delivery, and psychiatry) in which the nurse works. Also, the five remaining survey questions should be analyzed.

The influence of the other demographic variables should also be investigated. This may reveal the presence of lurking or confounding variables. A lurking variable is one that was not collected by the survey but has an influence on the relationship between EBP perception and organizational level. A potential lurking variable might be whether a nurse has previously worked at a magnet hospital. A confounding variable is one that is collected in the survey and has an influence on the relationship between EBP perception and organizational level. For example, all (or many) of the leaders may be older while many of the nurse professionals may be younger. In this situation organizational level is confounded with age. More advanced multivariate methods such as factor analysis may yield additional insight into the perception of EBP in the nursing workforce.

When interpreting the results you should be mindful of the limitations in the survey. The responses represent a non-random sample and the overall response rate was only 30%. Since this was a voluntary survey, self-selection bias may be present. It is possible that the nurses who chose to respond may be more engaged in EBP or hold stronger opinions about its implementation at the hospital. It is interesting to note that 18% of the nurses did not respond to these two survey questions. This suggests these nurses may be concerned about how the survey data will be used or that their responses can be personally identified from the demographic information. Despite these concerns, the survey and this analysis provide valuable information that could be used to advance the hospital's goal of achieving magnet designation.

Data Definitions

Primary Role	Job title: nurse manager/associate nurse manager/nurse educator or quality specialist/ registered nurse
Years of Service	Number of years employed as a nurse at this hospital
Org Level	Organizational level is either Leader or Nurse Professional
Employment status	Full-time/part-time/per diem
Education	Highest nursing degree held
Acute inpatient care unit	Hospital unit where the nurse works
EBP Favorability	Aggregation of responses to the question "All of the practice changes so far have been practical and fit well with the workflow of the unit." Favorable contains the agree and strongly agree responses, Unfavorable contains strongly disagree, disagree and neutral
Practicality & Workflow 3 point	Aggregation of responses to the question "Evidence based practice does not take into account the limitations of my practice setting." Agreement contains the agree and strongly agree responses, Disagreement contains strongly disagree, disagree and neutral

Problems

1 Consider the two survey questions that pertain to resources to assist nurses with evidence-based practice: (a) Literature and research findings are useful in my daily practice, and (b) There is sufficient information available for me to access when I have questions about the practice change. Analyze the nurses' responses to these two questions using the methods presented in this case. Compare the nurses' responses to those of the two questions pertaining to implementing EBP on the unit that were analyzed in the case.

2 Create a summary table showing the responses for all seven rating questions by organization level using Tabulate. Include both counts and percentages within each organization level (nurse professionals and nurse leaders).

3 Repeat the analysis shown in this case for survey questions of your choice. Prepare a few presentation slides that summarize your findings.

4 The non-response analysis showed that nurse leaders responded to the survey in greater proportion than did the nurse professionals in comparison to their occurrence in the hospital's nursing population. Discuss possible reasons for this and how it influences your interpretation of the results.

References

Stevens, Kathleen R., "The Impact of Evidence-Based Practice in Nursing and the Next Big Ideas," The Online Journal of Issues in Nursing, Vol. 18, No.2, May 2013, accessed on November 9, 2015 at http://nursingworld.org/MainMenuCategories/ANAMarketplace/ANAPeriodicals/OJIN/TableofContents/Vol-18-2013/No2-May-2013/Impact-of-Evidence-Based-Practice.html?css=print.

Gale BVP and Schaffer MA, "Organizational readiness for evidence-based practice," Journal of Nursing Administration, 2009; 39(2):91-97.

4

Health Care Costs Associated with Smoking: A National Perspective

Chapter Summary Concepts

Statistical Concepts	Data Management Concepts	JMP Features
Data Visualization • Geographic map	Metadata	Importing Excel files
	Database normalized form	Tables > Split
		Column Properties > Notes
		Graph Builder
		Annotate Tool

Background

The first link between smoking and lung cancer was reported in 1912 by American physician Isaac Adler. In the 1960s, the US Surgeon General began publishing annual reports detailing the health consequences of smoking. Since that time many measures have been taken by both the public and private sectors to reduce the health and economic consequences of smoking. These measures have included banning tobacco advertising on television, raising cigarette taxes, promoting anti-smoking education in schools, restricting smoking in public places, and providing assistance for those seeking to quit smoking. Currently, the economic impact of smoking-related illness exceeds $300 billion annually in the US with $170 billion attributable to direct medical care and over $156 billion attributable to lost productivity.

A California public health nurse is preparing educational material for a smoking cessation class. The focus of the unit she is preparing is the economic impact of smoking. The nurse is particularly interested in emphasizing the magnitude of the health care costs.

Problem Statement

Create data visualizations to show U.S. health care expenditures by state.

The Data

The Centers for Disease Control and Prevention maintain the State Tobacco Activities Tracking and Evaluation (STATE) System (https://www.cdc.gov/statesystem/) which contains a wealth of data related to the health and economic consequences associated with smoking. The Custom Reports feature was used to download the ambulatory, hospital, nursing home, prescription drug, other health care costs, and total cost for each US state and the District of Columbia. The annual data was available for the years 2005-2009. The file SmokingHealthcareExpenditures.xls, which contains the 2009 data, was downloaded from the STATE System.

Data Management

Importing an Excel File in JMP

Opening an Excel file in JMP will activate the Excel Import Wizard (Figure 4.1 on page 50), which allows you to control which worksheets are imported and to make adjustments such as selecting the number of rows that contain the column headings. Examine the Data Preview to make sure the columns are delimited correctly.

Figure 4.1 *Excel Import Wizard Showing Cost of Smoking Data*

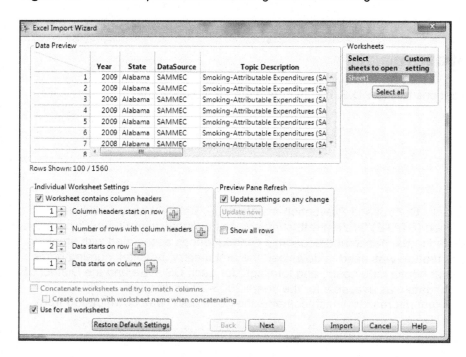

If there is more than one worksheet in the Excel file, select the sheets to import into JMP by highlighting them in the Worksheets portion of the Excel Import Wizard dialog. Once the data has been imported into JMP make sure that the data and modeling types are set appropriately for your analysis. For example, the "Data Value" column contains the smoking costs, which should be treated as a number. Right click in the "Data Value" column heading and select Column Info to view a dialog that shows the data and modeling types (See Figure 4.2 on page 50).

Figure 4.2 *Column Info Dialog*

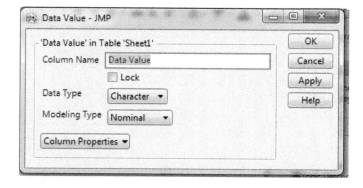

As imported from the Excel file, "Data Value" was formatted as character. Use the drop-down menus to change Data Type to Numeric and the Modeling Type to Continuous.

Splitting the "Data Value" Column

The STATE System exports the data in a format that is amenable to database operations. Some modifications will be required to facilitate JMP analysis.

For each state there are six rows corresponding to the six different types of health care expenses for 2009. This is a database normalized form that facilitates summing the different types of expenses and adding new categories of expenses. This is a best practice in database design as it allows flexibility in the number different types of expenses that are recorded.

JMP data sheets are designed to have variables in columns and observations in rows. For this analysis each type of expense should be in a separate column. This can be accomplished by selecting Tables >Split. Enter "Variable" into the Split By field, "Data Value" into the Split Columns field, and select the Keep All radio button. The completed dialog is shown in Figure 4.3 on page 51.

Figure 4.3   *Tables Split Dialog*

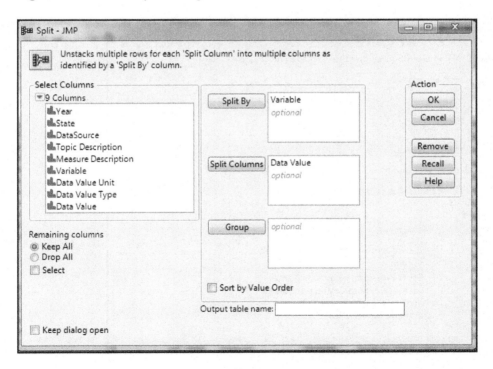

The JMP data table will now have a separate column for each type of expense.

Modifying the JMP Columns

The STATE System outputs several fields that specify the units, data source, and other metadata about the health care expenses. This method of documenting data values is a database management best practice. For example, merging the numeric value of expense and its units into one field would not allow mathematical operations to be performed.

Some of this metadata should be transferred to the JMP column headers, recorded as a JMP Column Property (Note) or included in the analysis narrative. The health care costs are given in millions of dollars and it is important that these units appear in the headings and legends of tables and graphs created from this data. This can be achieved by adding this information to the JMP column headings. Once incorporated into the JMP column headings, some of these metadata columns can be deleted.

The STATE system gives footnotes for the Other and Total expenditures. A JMP Note is a good place to retain this information. A Note can be attached to each column as a Column Property (right click on column name "Other Expense ($ mil) " > Column info> Column property> Notes), as shown in Figure 4.4 on page 52 for the Other expenditures.

Figure 4.4 *Adding Notes in the Column Properties Dialog*

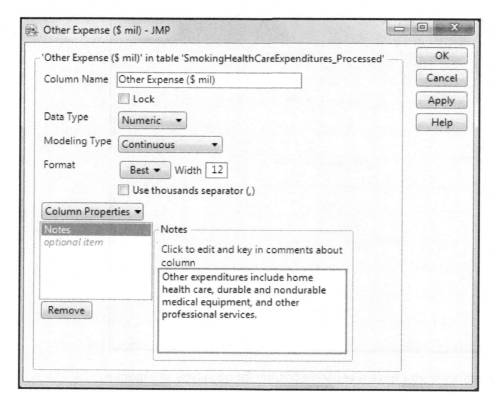

The edited file is saved in JMP format as SmokingHealthcareExpenditures.jmp. The new JMP column names are given in the Data Definition section of this case.

Analytic Approach

The three questions below will guide the selection of appropriate methods to create data visualizations to show U.S. health care expenditures by state.

1 What is the response (Y) of interest and how is it measured? The Total Healthcare Expense ($ mil) column aggregates all of the health care expenditures associated with smoking and will have the greatest impact for the smoking cessation class. It is likely that examining health care costs at a more granular level will not be as effective.

2 Are predictor variables mentioned in the problem statement? If so, how many and what are their measurement levels? There are no predictor variables identified in the problem statement.

3 What are you being asked to deliver? A data description, an interval estimate, an answer to a question, or a predictive model? We are being asked to give a data description. Geospatial data is easily assimilated when plotted on maps. This allows the audience to easily visualize geographic trends.

JMP Analysis

We begin our analysis with a histogram and box plot of Total Healthcare Expense ($ mil), obtained from the Distribution platform, as shown in Figure 4.5 on page 54.

Figure 4.5   *Histogram and Box Plot for Total Healthcare Expense ($ mil)*

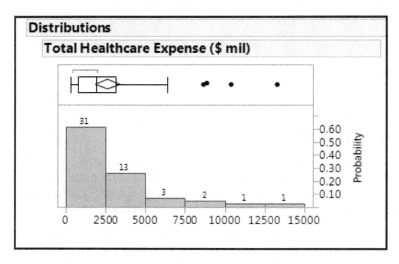

The distribution is right skewed with 31 (62%) of the states having total health care expenditures of less than $2500 million.

A heat map of the total health care expenditures can be created using JMP's Graph Builder. A heat map is an effective means to visualize geographic data and uses a color scale to represent the total health care expenditures for each state. Figure 4.6 on page 54 shows an empty Graph Builder dialog.

Figure 4.6   *Graph Builder Dialog*

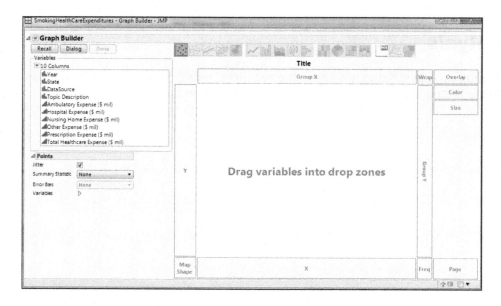

Drag State into the Map Shape drop zone and drag Total Healthcare Expense ($ mil) into the Color drop zone. JMP contains a library of map files located in the directory where JMP was installed. To use one of the built-in maps, the column describing the geographic region must match one of the formats given in the map shape file. For example, the US map shape file contains several columns with different designations for US states such as the full name (e.g., California), the United States Postal Service Code (e.g., CA) or the State FIPS code (e.g., 06). Figure 4.7 on page 55 shows the completed Graph Builder dialog.

Figure 4.7 *Graph Builder Dialog to Create a Heat Map of Total Healthcare Expense*

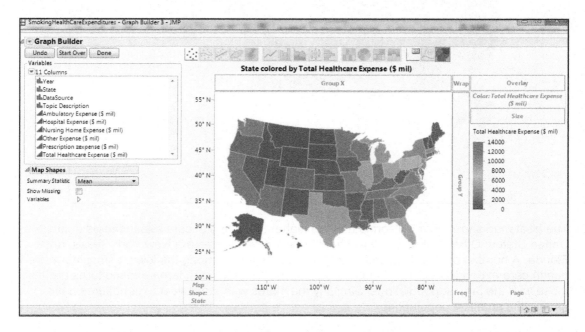

Click Done to view the final heat map of Total Healthcare Expense (Figure 4.8 on page 56).

Figure 4.8 Heat Map of Total Healthcare Expense

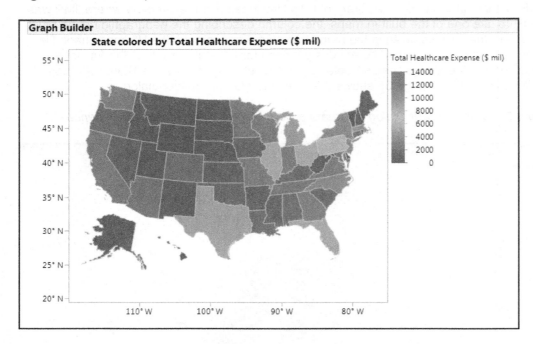

The heat map shows that California has the highest total health care expenditures in the United States. Other states with large health care expenditures are New York, Texas, and Florida. A number of New England and Plains states have among the lowest smoking-related health care expenditures. This is not surprising as the states with large expenditures are also those with the largest populations. Similarly the states with the lowest expenditures have among the smallest populations.

Analysis Implications

The heat map is an effective way to present the total health care expenditures by state. Public health data disseminated to the general public is often displayed on maps. This allows the data consumer to visually identify geographic patterns. To further illustrate the impact of smoking, the public health nurse may wish to report the total health care expenditures for the entire country.

For each state, total health care expenditures are related to the size of the population. Given the problem statement, this is appropriate as we are interested in the magnitude of smoking-related health care costs. In other situations, state health care expenditures should be adjusted for population size so that states can be compared equitably. In our next case we will continue our examination of smoking-related costs by comparing state investment in smoking cessation programs. This will require the use of adjusted measures.

Data Definitions

Year	2009
State	Full name of the US states
Data Source	Smoking-Attributable Mortality, Morbidity, and Economic Costs (SAMMEC)
Topic Description	Metadata
Ambulatory Expense ($ mil)	
Hospital Expense ($ mil)	
Nursing Home Expense ($ mil)	
Other Expense ($ mil)	Other expenditures include home health care, durable and nondurable medical equipment, and other professional services.
Prescription Expense ($ mil)	
Total Healthcare Expense ($ mil)	Excludes dental expenditure

Problems

1 Create heat maps for ambulatory, hospital, nursing home, and prescription expenses. Compare these heat maps and write a paragraph noting similarities, differences, and interesting or unusual patterns.

2 Prepare a single presentation slide that summarizes national smoking-related health care costs by selecting among the heat maps created in Problem 1. Enrich your map(s) using the Annotate tool to add context. Add an appropriate amount of narrative to the slide with the goal of demonstrating the economic impact of smoking.

3 The file CA_Counties.xlsx contains smoking-related information for the state of California by county. Create a heat map for the state of California for the Direct Costs. Which map, the national or state map, would you recommend to use for the smoking cessation class? Explain your reasoning.

4 The CDC (and other organizations that report health care information) frequently use estimation methods to obtain macro-level data such as the state-wide smoking-related health care costs used in this case. Why is this done? Why is it important for an analyst to understand the estimation method associated with such as data set?

References

"The Health Consequences of Smoking—50 Years of Progress: A Report of the Surgeon General, 2014," *http://www.surgeongeneral.gov/library/reports/50-years-of-progress/ #fullreport*, accessed September 1, 2016.

Max, W., H.Y. Sung, S. Yanling, B. Start, "The Cost of Smoking in California, 2009" Institute for Health & Aging, School of Nursing University of California, San Francisco.

5

Health Care Costs Associated with Smoking and Cessation Expenditures

Chapter Summary Concepts

Statistical Concepts	Data Management Concepts	JMP Features
Data Visualization • Geographic maps	Joining tables	Tables>Join
Descriptive Statistics	Units conversion	Formula Editor
Correlation		Tabulate
Correlation vs. causation		Graph Builder
		Multivariate Methods>Multivariate

Background

Government and health care organizations are engaged in a variety of strategies to reduce tobacco use with the goal of decreasing health care costs and improving population health. The economic impact of smoking-related illness exceeds $300 billion annually in the US with $170 billion attributable to direct medical care and over $156 billion attributable to lost productivity. The Centers for Disease Control reported over 480,000 deaths in the US in 2016 due to smoking and the effects of second hand smoke. The World Health Organization issued policy recommendations in 2003 with three strategies to reduce tobacco use:

■ A public health approach that seeks to change the social climate and promote a supportive environment;

■ A health systems approach that focuses on promoting and integrating clinical best practices (behavioral and pharmacological) which help tobacco-dependent consumers increase their chance of quitting successfully;

■ A surveillance, research and information approach that promotes the exchange of information and knowledge so as to increase awareness of the need to change social norms.[1]

A California public health nurse is preparing educational material for a smoking cessation class. In the case "Health Care Costs Associated with Smoking: A National Perceptive," a heat map was created that shows the total cost of health care for each state. A heat map is an effective way to visualize this data. As the nurse continues to prepare for the class, she is interested in examining expenditure data from state government programs and policies aimed at smoking cessation.

Problem Statement

Create data visualizations to show US expenditures for smoking cessation by state and examine associations between expenditures for smoking cessation programs and smoking-related health care and demographic factors.

The Data

We will expand the data set (SmokingHealthCareExpenditures.jmp) from the case "Health Care Costs Associated with Smoking: A National Perceptive," to include additional data on smoking cessation expenditures, cigarette taxes, median household income, population, land area, and other demographic information for each US state. The data was obtained from the Centers for Disease Control's State Tobacco Activities Tracking and Evaluation (STATE) System and the US Census Bureau (www.census.gov) and compiled into the file SmokingDeterranceAndDemographics.jmp.

Data Management

Joining Two JMP Data Tables

To combine the two data tables into a single data table, begin by opening both SmokingHealthcareExpenditures.jmp and SmokingDeterranceAndDemographics.jmp. The State columns in each data table must be the same list of values for the join to execute properly. In our case, both State columns contain the full name of each State (e.g., Alabama, New York, etc.) and therefore will join correctly. There are two components of a join: how

---

1   "Policy Recommendations for Smoking Cessation and Treatment of Tobacco Dependence," World Health Organization, 2003, http://www.who.int/tobacco/resources/publications/tobacco_dependence/en/, accessed August 25, 2017.

many rows are retained and how the records are matched. In this instance we are choosing an inner join as it returns all rows where there is a match and also an equijoin, as the operator that is used to match the rows is equality. The two data tables will be joined by matching the "State" columns where the State values are equal. Click on the data table SmokingHealthcareExpenditures.jmp to make it the active window. Select Tables > Join and highlight the fields as shown in Figure 5.1 on page 62. In the "Output table name" field enter "SmokingCostsCombined" as the name of the new table.

Figure 5.1   *Completed Join Dialog*

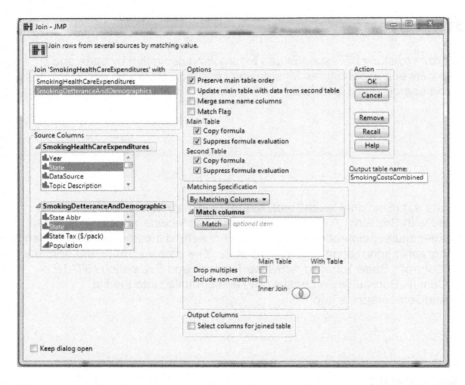

Click on the Match button to enter that the "State" columns as the matching columns. The result is shown in Figure 5.2 on page 63.

Figure 5.2 *Tables>Join Dialog after Selecting the Matching Columns*

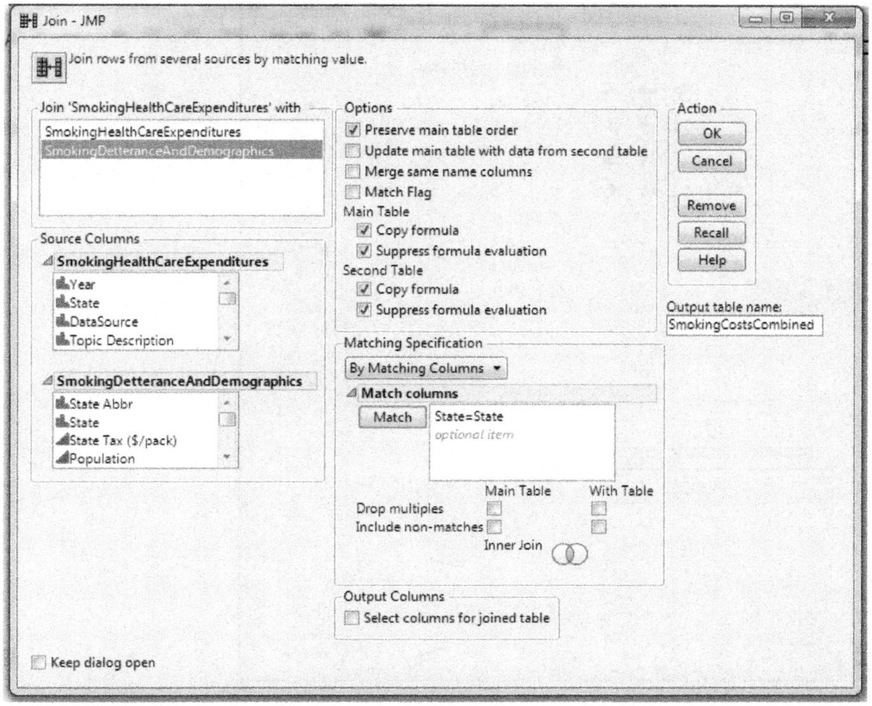

Click the OK button to join the two data tables into the single table SmokingCostsCombined.jmp. See the Data Definitions section for an explanation of the columns contained in this file.

Creating a New Column Using the Formula Editor

In the case "Health Care Costs Associated with Smoking: A National Perceptive," a heat map of total health care expenses suggested that states with larger populations had larger total health care expenses. This is to be expected as larger populations will have more smokers and hence more smoking-related costs. To compare states of different population sizes equitably, we can adjust the health care expenditures for population size. This can be done by creating new columns with the formula editor. To create total health care expenditures adjusted for state population, navigate to the last column in the data table and double click to the right to add a new column. Double click on the column header and enter the column name "Adjusted Total Healthcare Expense ($ mil/capita)" then right click and select Formula. Enter the formula as shown in Figure 5.3 on page 64.

Figure 5.3 *Formula to Create Adjusted Total Healthcare Expenditures*

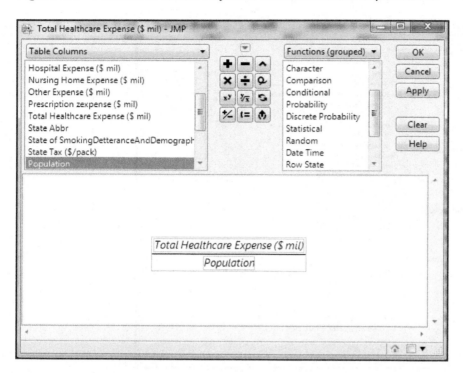

Click OK to create the population adjusted total health care expense. Figure 5.4 on page 64 shows the first few rows of the data table now containing adjusted total health care expense.

Figure 5.4 *Sample of Adjusted Total Healthcare Expense Values*

	BEA Region	Median Household ...	Cessation Expenditures ($)	Land Area	Adjusted Total Healthcare Expense ($ mil/capita)
1	Southeast	40489	282000	50645	0.0004004708
2	Far West	66953	2010000	570641	0.0006272254
3	Southwest	48745	3905000	113594	0.0003612917
4	Southeast	37825	4272000	52035	0.0004205299
5	Far West	58931	5157000	155779	0.0003596267
6	Rocky Mountain	55430	5900000	103642	0.0003764368
7	New England	67034	3839000	4842	0.0005794864

After creating a new formula always examine the result. Notice that the units of millions of dollars per capita is not intuitive. When reporting total health care expense per capita, units of dollars per person would be more easily understood. Modify the formula as shown in Figure 5.5 on page 65 to change the units to dollars per capita.

Figure 5.5 *Formula to Create Adjusted Total Healthcare Expense in Units of $/capita*

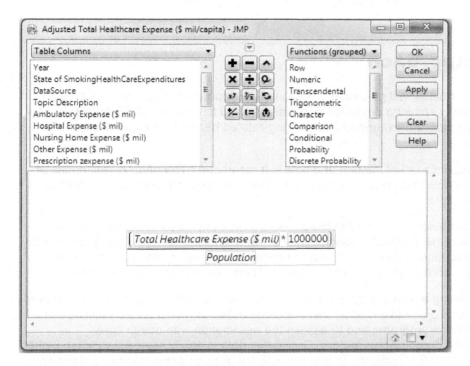

Modify the column name to reflect the units of dollars per capita.

Examining summary statistics is a good practice to check if the values obtained from the formula make sense in the context of the problem. Figure 5.6 on page 65 shows summary statistics generated from the Tabulate platform.

Figure 5.6 *Summary Statistics for Total Healthcare Expenditures ($/capita)*

Tabulate

	Adjusted Total Healthcare Expense ($/capita)
N	51
Mean	459.08
Std Dev	88.39
Min	194.75
Max	652.04

Across the United States the average annual cost per person for smoking-related health care costs is $459.08. An internet search can quickly validate the reasonableness of this per capita average. The column Cessation Expenditures ($) should also be adjusted to a per capita basis.

Analytic Approach

The three questions below will guide the selection of appropriate methods to create data visualizations to show smoking cessation expenditures and to assess associations between smoking cessation program expenditures, smoking-related health care expenditures, and demographic factors.

1 What is the response (Y) of interest and how is it measured? The primary responses of interest are total health care expenditures and cessation expenditures. Both of these are continuous variables.

2 Are predictor variables mentioned in the problem statement? If so, how many and what are their measurement levels? Associations between smoking-related expenditures and the demographic factors land area, median household income, state gross domestic product, and tobacco production are of interest. These are all continuous variables.

3 What are you being asked to deliver? A data description, an interval estimate, an answer to a question, or a predictive model? We are being asked to give a data description of smoking prevention programs and to assess the association with health care expenditures and demographic factors. Geospatial data is easily assimilated when plotted on maps and allows the audience to identify regional or geographic trends. Correlation analysis can be conducted to quantify the association between pairs of continuous variables.

JMP Analysis

Descriptive Analysis

Every analysis should begin by describing the data. Figure 5.7 on page 67 through Figure 5.9 on page 67 show summary statistics for the data grouped by health care expenditures, cessation expenditures, and demographic factors. These tables were produced from the Tabulate platform.

Figure 5.7   *Summary Statistics for State Health Care Expenditures*

	N	Mean	Std Dev	Min	Max
Ambulatory Expense ($ mil)	51	397.759	464.300	32.400	2546.600
Hospital Expense ($ mil)	51	1357.971	1393.795	149.700	6726.400
Nursing Home Expense ($ mil)	51	204.788	212.037	9.700	912.600
Other Expense ($ mil)	51	161.635	188.330	14.400	907.100
Prescription expense ($ mil)	51	494.308	530.446	41.500	2391.300
Total Healthcare Expense ($ mil)	51	2616.457	2755.838	257.700	13292.400
Adjusted Total Healthcare Expense ($/capita)	51	459.080	88.390	194.752	652.039
Adjusted Cessation Expense ($/capita)	51	0.865	0.889	0.022	3.921

Figure 5.8   *Summary Statistics for State Smoking Cessation Expenditures*

	N	Mean	Std Dev	Min	Max
State Tax ($/pack)	51	1.19	0.74	0.07	2.75
Cessation Expenditures ($)	51	2698216	3150266	100000	20936000
Adjusted Cessation Expense ($/capita)	51	0.865	0.889	0.022	3.921

Figure 5.9   *Summary Statistics for State Demographic Factors*

	N	Mean	Std Dev	Min	Max
Population	51	6019736	6780646	544270	36961664
State GDP ($mil)	51	274801	330959	24625	1847048
Median Household Income	51	60471	72782	36646	566616
Land Area	51	69253	85526	61	570641

Tobacco Producer	N	% of Total
No	34	66.7%
Yes	17	33.3%
BEA Region		
.	1	2.0%
Far West	6	11.8%
Great Lakes	5	9.8%
Mideast	6	11.8%
New England	6	11.8%
Plains	6	11.8%
Rocky Mountain	5	9.8%
Southeast	12	23.5%
Southwest	4	7.8%

Summary tables such as these are frequently found in technical reports and journal articles. They acquaint the reader with the data that was collected. Grouping variables into separate tables by category makes it easier for the reader to assimilate the information.

Heat Maps for Cessation Expenditures

Heat maps are effective for presenting geographic information and are easily created with Graph Builder. To create a heat map for Cessation Expenditures ($), drag State into the Map Shape drop zone and drag Cessation Expenditures ($) into the Color drop zone. JMP contains a library of map files located in the directory where JMP was installed. To use one of the built-in maps, the column describing the geographic region must match one of the formats given in the map shape file. For example, the US map shape file contains several columns with different designations for US states such as the full name (e.g., California), the United States Postal Service Code (e.g., CA) or the State FIPS code (e.g., 06). Figure 5.10 on page 68 shows a heat map for the total cessation expenditures by state.

Figure 5.10 *Heat Map of Cessation Expenditures by State*

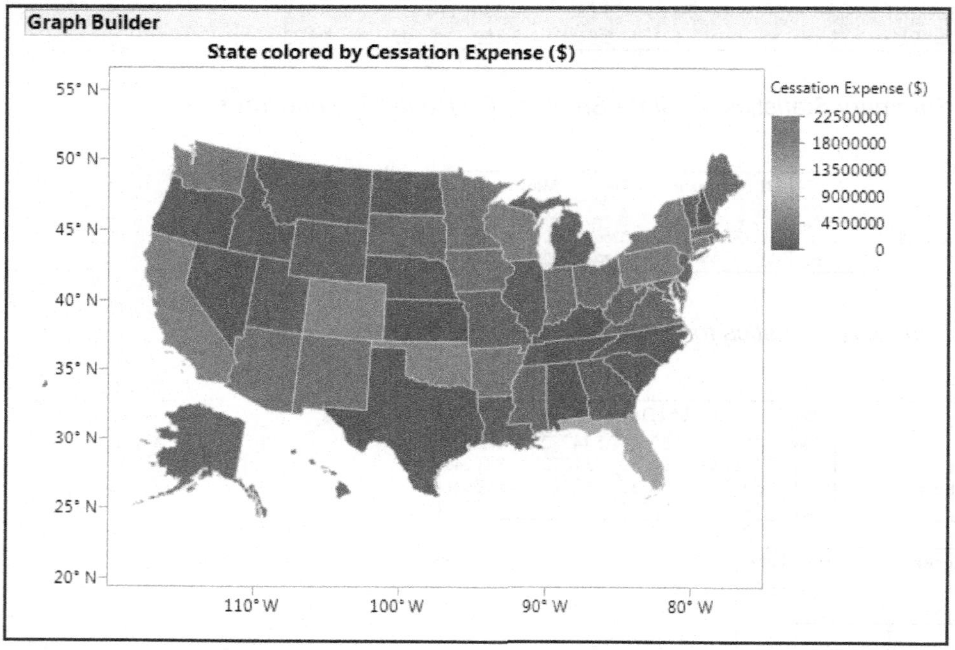

In this heat map we see that New York State spends considerably more on cessation programs than any other state. Other states with large populations such as Florida and California also spend larger amounts on smoking cessation than less populated states, but this is not universally true. Oklahoma and Colorado as examples of less populated states that spend relatively large amounts on smoking cessation. This suggests that factors other than population size play a role in determining cessation expenditures. This pattern is different than what we observed using the heat map of total health care expenses created in the case "Health Care Costs Associated with Smoking: A National Perceptive."

A heat map for cessation expenses per capita was created in a similar manner and is shown in Figure 5.11 on page 69.

Figure 5.11 *Heat Map of Cessation Expense per Capita by State*

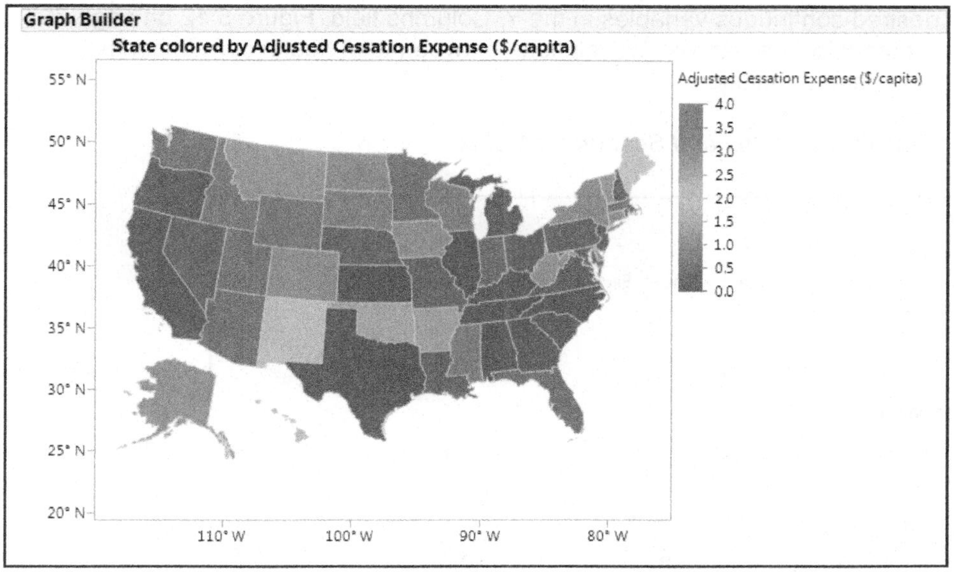

The heat map of the per capita cessation expense shows a different pattern compared to the state total cessation expense. New York no longer leads the nation in cessation expenditures when viewed on a per capita basis. Colorado is now the leading state. Texas' spending on smoking cessation was relatively low on both a per capita and total basis. This suggests that factors other than population size are considered in a state's determination of how much of its resources to allocate to smoking cessation programs. The heat maps shown here are useful to the analyst for exploring the data, postulating more detailed research questions, and choosing further analyses to perform.

Correlation Analysis

Correlation analysis quantifies the linear association between two continuous variables. The correlation coefficient measures this linear association of a scale from -1 to 1 and expresses two aspects of the relationship. The sign of the correlation coefficient tells us whether there is a direct or inverse relationship between the two variables. The correlation coefficient for a direct relationship will have a positive sign while the correlation coefficient for an inverse relationship will have a negative sign. A correlation coefficient of 0 indicates that there is no relationship between the two variables. The correlation coefficient also describes the strength of the relationship. A larger correlation coefficient, in absolute value, indicates are stronger relationship, while a relatively smaller correlation coefficient indicates a weaker relationship. Examining the correlation coefficient helps the analyst describe the direction and strength of the relationships between two continuous variables. Correlation between two variables does not imply a causal relationship. For example, population size does not cause smoking-related health care costs. Smoking is caused by factors such as youthful experimentation, stress, or family history. The magnitude of state health care costs is associated with state population.

Correlation coefficients can be calculated using the JMP Multivariate Methods platform. To view a matrix of correlation coefficients, select Analyze > Multivariate Methods > Multivariate and enter the desired continuous variables in the Y, Columns field. Figure 5.12 on page 70 shows the JMP output for the pairwise correlations between total health care expense, cessation expense, and population.

Figure 5.12 *Correlation Matrix and Scatterplot Matrix*

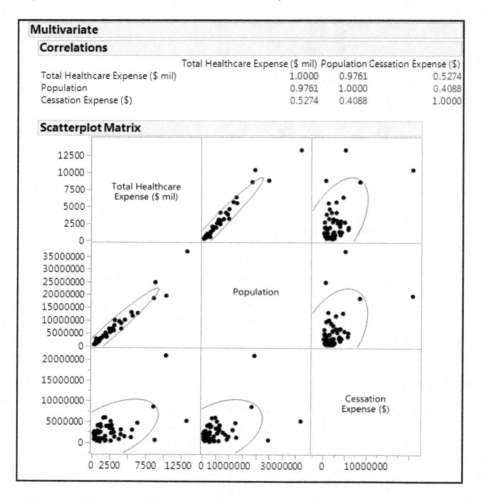

Both total health care expense and cessation expense are directly associated with population size. Total health care expense and population size have a correlation coefficient of 0.9761 and cessation expense and population size have a correlation coefficient of 0.4088. Total health care is more strongly correlated to population size. This makes sense as a larger population will have more smokers and hence more smoking-related health care expenditures. Cessation expenditures are likely influenced by factors besides population size such as state public health priorities and policies.

The scatterplot matrix shows the relationships visually and allows outliers to be identified. The data points on the scatterplot for total health care expense and population size are tightly coupled as compared to the scatterplot for cessation expense and population size. Cessation expense and total health care expense have a modest correlation of 0.5274. In the associated scatterplot matrix, California, Texas, and New York, three large population states, appear to be outliers.

Other correlations can be similarly calculated from the remaining continuous variable given in the data set such as land area, state gross domestic product, and state cigarette taxes. For example, there is a direct and modest correlation of 0.491 between state cigarette tax and adjusted total health care expense. The correlation between state cigarette tax and total health care expense is quite close to zero at 0.088.

Analysis Implications

In this case we have explored the use of heat maps as an effective means to visualize geographic data. The impressions drawn from the heat maps of cessation expense and cessation expense adjusted for population size are quite different. The choice of which visualization is most appropriate depends on the problem statement and the important messages to be conveyed to your audience. In the smoking cessation class, where only a few graphs and statistics would be desired, the heat maps showing total health care expense and total cessation expense communicates the nationwide magnitude of the health care costs associated with smoking and the efforts being made to prevent smoking. The average total health care cost per capita of $459 per person is another powerful statistic in illustrating smoking related costs.

Correlation analysis quantifies the relationship between continuous variables both in terms of direction and strength of association. Examining correlations can also help identify when adjusted values should be reported. For example, the strong relationship between total health care expense and population size suggests that when comparing these expenses between states, a value adjusted for population size should be reported. Always bear in mind that a correlation established from data does not imply that one variable causes another. Causality must be determined from other evidence found in the problem domain. Interpreting correlations between adjusted and unadjusted variables can be difficult. Finally, only a few of the possible analyses have been presented in this case. There are many more relationships that can be explored from this relatively small data set. Considerable time is required to fully explore the relationships between the relatively small number of variables and to examine the various ways in which the data can be summarized and visualized. It is important to choose only those data visualizations and statistics that will resonate with the audience and communicate the intended message in the time allotted.

Data Definitions

Year	2009
State	Full name of the US state
Data Source	Smoking-Attributable Mortality, Morbidity, and Economic Costs (SAMMEC)
Topic Description	Metadata
Ambulatory Expense ($ mil)	
Hospital Expense ($ mil)	
Nursing Home Expense ($ mil)	
Other Expense ($ mil)	Other expenditures include home health care, durable and nondurable medical equipment, and other professional services.
Prescription Expense ($ mil)	
Total Healthcare Expense ($ mil)	Excludes dental expenditure
State Tax ($/pack)	State tax levied on a pack of cigarettes
Population	State population in 2009
State GDP ($ mil)	State gross domestic product in millions of dollars. This is a measure of the state's economic output.
BEA Region	US geographic regions as defined by the US Bureau of Economic Analysis
Median Household Income	In $ for 2009

| Cessation Expenditures ($) | Total state expenditures on smoking cessation programs such as education, advertising, and subsidies for smoking cessation medications. |

| Land area | State land area in square miles |

Adjusted Total Healthcare Expense ($/capita)

Adjusted Cessation Expense ($/capita)

Problems

1 Create a heat map of state cigarette taxes. What patterns do you observe from this map?

2 Explore the relationship between state gross domestic product (GDP) and cessation expense. Is the claim that states with greater economic output spend more on cessation programs supported by the data? Adjust state GDP for population size. This will give the economic output on a per capita basis. Do you think these two variables should be compared using adjusted or unadjusted values? Explain your reasoning using correlation coefficients.

3 Search the Internet for examples where smoking related data is presented. Select two examples and critique the data presentation in the context of the intended audience.

Reference

"The Health Consequences of Smoking—50 Years of Progress: A Report of the Surgeon General, 2014," http://www.surgeongeneral.gov/library/reports/50-years-of-progress/#fullreport, accessed September 1, 2016.

"Policy Recommendations for Smoking Cessation and Treatment of Tobacco Dependence," World Health Organization, 2003, http://www.who.int/tobacco/resources/publications/tobacco_dependence/en/, accessed August 25, 2017.

6

Creatinine Levels in Hospitalized Patients

Chapter Summary Concepts

Statistical Concepts	Data Management Concepts	JMP Features
Descriptive statistics	Data coding	Distribution
Test of hypothesis	Codebook	Recode
Confidence interval		Tabulate
Testing assumptions		JMP Data and Modeling Types
Data visualization		Formula Editor
• Histogram		
• Normal Quantile Plot		

Background

Creatinine is produced continuously by the normal breakdown of muscle tissues. Kidneys filter creatinine which is excreted into urine. Blood tests for creatinine measure kidney function with high levels indicating poor kidney function. The normal range for creatinine is 0.84 to 1.21 milligrams per deciliter (mg/dL), but this can vary based on gender and age. Creatinine levels can temporarily be elevated due to dehydration, recent red meat consumption, and certain medications. Creatinine levels from 1.6 – 2.0 indicate Stage 1 kidney insufficiency. Acute Kidney Injury (AKI) is a sudden decrease in kidney function within a few hours or days. AKI is common in hospitalized patients, especially the elderly and those in intensive care.

In this case study we examine medical conditions, creatinine levels, and demographic factors for a sample of patients who have been treated at a hospital.

Problem Statement

To what extent does this group of patients that are treated at a hospital present with kidney insufficiency? The research questions are:

1 On average do creatinine levels exceed the upper endpoint (2 mg/dL) of the Stage 1 kidney insufficiency range?

2 What proportion of patients have creatinine levels greater than 2 mg/dL?

The Data

Data was obtained from the Integrating Data for Analysis, Anonymization and SHaring (iDASH) website[1] for 372 hospital patients. The data for this case is synthetic, as it is difficult to obtain open-source patient-level medical information due to privacy concerns. The file CreatinineLevels.jmp contains the creatinine levels for these patients along with length of hospital stay, the presence of selected medical conditions, and demographic factors. Notice that the disease variables are "coded" meaning that numeric values are used to indicate the presence or absence of a disease. Similarly, the race category is coded in three levels. The variables and associated codes for this data set are given in the Data Definitions section.

Data Management

Introduction

Why is the data coded? Doesn't it seem easier to use words that are more descriptive (i.e., diabetes, no diabetes)? There are a number of reasons why data collections, particularly large ones, are coded. Some computer programs, such as Excel, have limited capability for processing alphanumerics. When data is collected on paper (such as from questionnaires), it is more efficient and less error prone to transcribe the data into electronic form using codes. Oftentimes, these codes are assigned from a domain list of values within the collection

---

1 The iDASH repository (https://idash-data.ucsd.edu) is supported by the National Institutes of Health through the NIH Roadmap for Medical Research, Grant U54HL108460.

process, by choosing the corresponding textual definition of the code. Large data collections are often accompanied by a codebook which gives the variable and code definitions.

While coded data is efficient for information processing, it is not ideal when communicating statistical results to stakeholders. Therefore we will "decode" the data prior to analysis.

Setting the JMP Modeling Type

Level (or scale) of measurement describes the relationship between the values that a variable can assume. The values of a nominal variable represent different categories, for example, gender or geographic region. An ordinal variable's values have an implied ordering, such as in a severity of illness rating with levels minor, moderate, major, and extreme. An interval scale applies to numeric variables where intervals have the same interpretation throughout the scale, such as with temperature. Ratio scales have an absolute zero, for example, currency or age. A JMP modeling type is assigned to each column to indicate the level of measurement for that variable. There are three modeling types: nominal, ordinal, and numeric. The numeric type is assigned to variables measured on an interval or ordinal scale.

By default, JMP assigns a modeling type of continuous to columns containing numbers. It is important to assign JMP columns the proper modeling type so that the appropriate statistical analysis will be performed. All of the columns in CreatinineLevels.jmp are initially set to have a continuous modeling type. The patient_id column contains a unique anonymized patient identification number and should be assigned a nominal modeling type. To change the modeling type, right click at the patient_id icon in the column list on the left of the data table and select "nominal" as shown in Figure 6.1 on page 78.

Figure 6.1   *Changing Modeling Type*

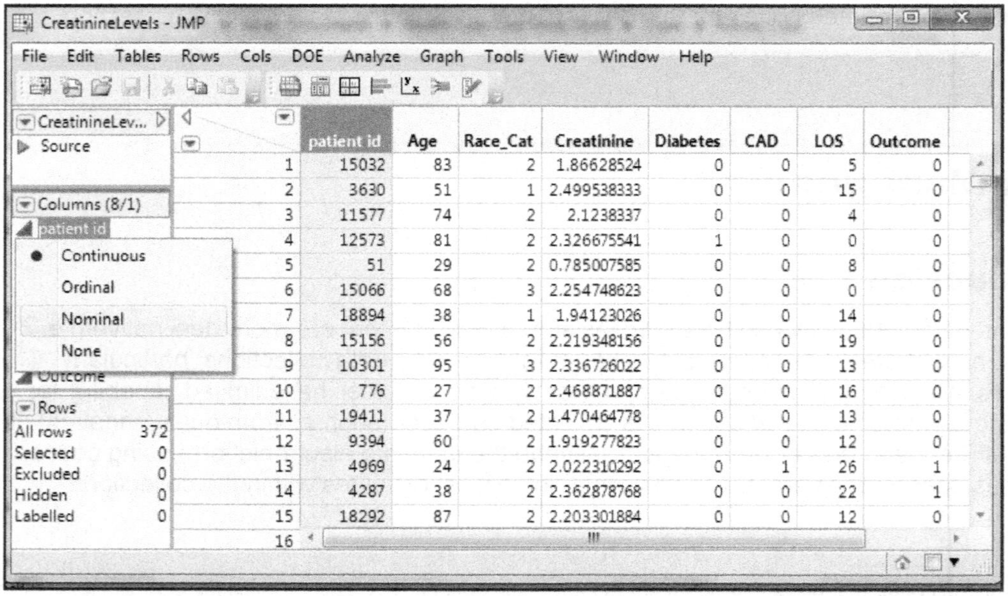

Notice that the icon for patient_id now appears as a small red histogram.

Renaming the Coded Variable Levels

The columns Diabetes, CAD, Outcome, and Race_Cat are all coded nominal variables. They will be easier to interpret if they are decoded into more descriptive names. The columns associated with the presence of disease are examples of binary or indicator variables, which are nominal variables with two possible values. It is conventional to assign a value of 0 when the disease is absent and a value of 1 when the disease is present. These variable levels can be easily renamed with the Recode feature selected from the Cols menu using the option "In Place" to replace the codes with descriptive names. The completed Recode dialog for Diabetes is shown in Figure 6.2 on page 79.

Figure 6.2   *Recoding the Diabetes Column*

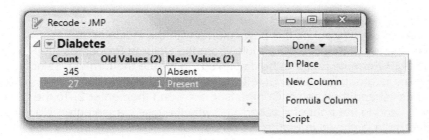

The same recoding is completed for CAD and Outcome; the same technique can be applied to the Race_Cat column. (See Data Definitions section for the decoded values.)

Creating and Populating a Column

The data set does not contain a variable that allows us to directly estimate the proportion of patients with creatinine level greater than 2. A new variable containing an indicator variable can easily be created. When a variable is created from existing data it is referred to as derived data.

To estimate the proportion of patients that have a creatinine level greater than 2, create a column that contains a nominal variable that will serve as an indicator. Add a new column by double clicking in the blank column header to the right of the Outcome column. Right click and select Column Info from the menu. Figure 6.3 on page 80 shows the completed dialog where a descriptive column name has been added.

Figure 6.3   *Setting the Column Name and Data and Modeling Types*

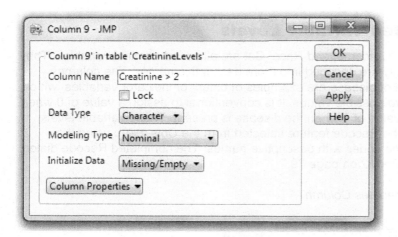

The JMP Formula Editor allows us to populate this new column with the indicator corresponding to the creatinine level. Selecting "Formula" from the Column Properties drop-down menu will cause the JMP Formula Editor to be displayed. To create the formula, select Conditional > If from the formula group list at the far left. In the expression box add Creatinine from the Columns list and then select Comparison > => and then enter 2. To the right of the = enter "Stage 1" and to the right of = associated with the else clause enter "No disease". The completed formula is shown in Figure 6.4 on page 81.

Figure 6.4 *Creating Values in a New Column Using the Formula Editor*

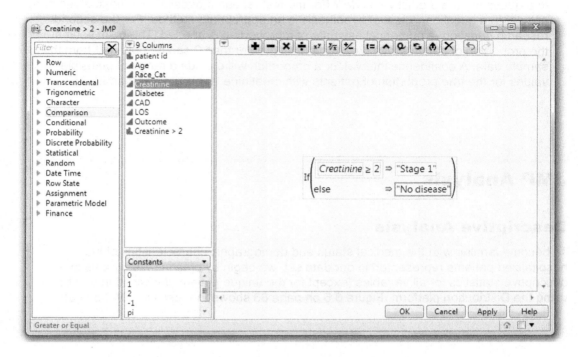

Apply the formula to the new column. The assignment of character values will cause the column to have a character data type and a nominal modeling type. The data file is now ready for analysis.

Analytic Approach

The problem statement poses two research questions: "On average do creatinine levels exceed the upper endpoint (2 mg/dL) of the Stage 1 kidney insufficiency range?" and "What proportion of patients have creatinine levels greater than 2 mg/dL?" The three questions below will guide the selection of appropriate statistical methods.

1 What is the response (Y) of interest and how is it measured? For the first research question, the creatinine level is of interest. It is a continuous variable. For the second research question, the nominal variable indicating creatinine level greater than two should be analyzed.

2 Are predictor variables mentioned in the problem statement? If so, how many and what are their measurement levels? There are no predictor variables mentioned in the research questions.

3 What are you being asked to deliver? A data description, an interval estimate, an answer to a question, or a predictive model? For the first research question, we need a yes or no answer to a question. A test of hypothesis is an appropriate method. For the second research question, a numerical estimate of a proportion is needed. The point estimate of the proportion of patients with creatinine level greater than 2 can be obtained from the sample data. A confidence interval for a proportion will provide a range of plausible values for the true proportion of patients with creatinine levels greater than 2.

JMP Analysis

Descriptive Analysis

To become familiar with the medical status and demographic characteristics of the hospitalized patients represented in our data set, we begin by creating histograms and descriptive statistics for all variables (except for the unique patient identification numbers) using the Distribution platform. Figure 6.5 on page 83 shows the resulting JMP output.

Figure 6.5 *Histograms and Summary Statistics from Distribution Platform*

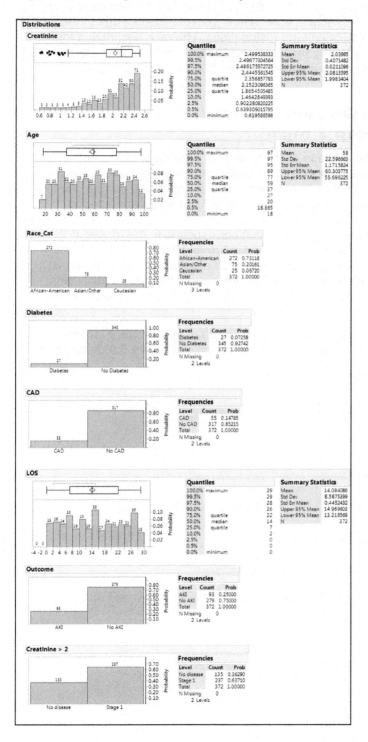

The creatinine distribution is left-skewed; 63.7% of the patients have creatinine levels greater than 2 mg/dL. The mean creatinine level is 2.04 while the median is 2.15 with values ranging from 0.62 to 2.50 mg/dL. The mean creatinine level is less than the median due to the left skew. Age and length of stay show fairly uniform distributions. The race distribution for this data set is 73% African-American, 20% Asian/Other, and 7% Caucasian. For these patients, 7% have diabetes, 15% have coronary artery disease, and 25% have acute kidney injury.

Research Question 1: On average do creatinine levels exceed 2 mg/dL?

The research question specifies the average as the statistical parameter of interest. The sample mean for creatinine level is 2.04 and is quite close to the hypothesized value of two. A one-sample t test is an appropriate method to determine if the observed sample mean is significantly different from hypothesized value or if the difference can be attributed to sampling error. In this research question, the null hypothesis is that the true mean creatinine level equals two. A one-sided alternative (greater than) corresponds to the research question. Alternative hypotheses are in two forms, one-sided and two-sided; the choice depends on how the research question is posed. Two-sided alternatives are appropriate when testing for equality with the hypothesized value. One-sided alternatives apply when discovering a difference from the hypothesized value in only one direction (greater than or less than) is of interest.

The one-sample t-test can be conducted from the JMP Distribution platform. From the drop-down menu select Test Mean and complete the dialog as shown in Figure 6.6 on page 84.

Figure 6.6 *Test Mean Dialog for Creatinine Level*

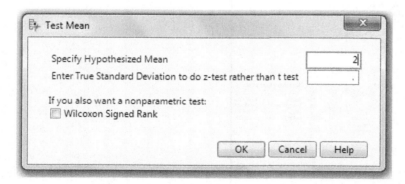

The Test Mean output is added to the default Distribution output as shown in Figure 6.7 on page 85.

Figure 6.7 *Test Mean Output for Creatinine Level*

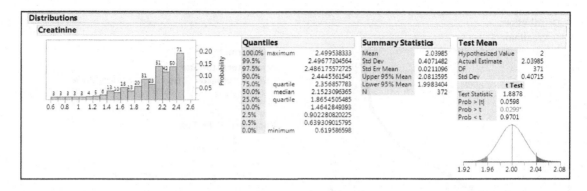

The p-value is the key result from a hypothesis test. Since we are interested in determining if the mean creatinine level exceeds 2, "Prob > t" is the correct p-value. A p-value expresses the likelihood of obtaining the sample mean or something more extreme assuming the null hypothesis is true. Small p-values cause a rejection of the null hypothesis. The significance level is the risk of rejecting the null hypothesis when it is in fact true. A p-value less than the chosen significance level means that the null hypothesis is rejected. For this test we'll choose a significance level of 0.05. The p-value of 0.0299 is less than 0.05, hence the null hypothesis is rejected in favor of the alternative. The test tells us that the mean creatinine level is significantly larger than 2.

The assumptions of a one-sample t-test are random sampling and that the population is normally distributed. Creatinine does not appear normally distributed based on visual inspection of the histogram in Figure 6.7 on page 85. The normality assumption for Creatinine can be formally assessed from the JMP Distribution platform in two different ways. Figure 6.8 on page 86 shows a normal quantile plot for Creatinine obtained from the Creatinine drop-down menu.

Figure 6.8   *Normal Quantile Plot and Shapiro-Wilks Normality Test Output for Creatinine*

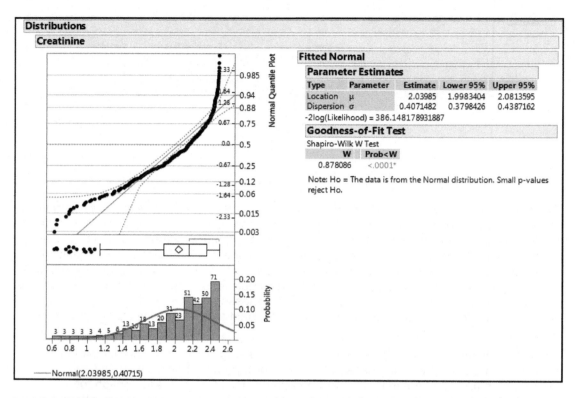

In the Normal quantile plot, the line corresponds to the Normal distribution that best fits the data. The normality assumption is satisfied to the extent that the observations lie close to this line. The observed Creatinine values show considerable departure from the line. The JMP Distribution platform also provides the Shapiro-Wilk normality test as an option. From the Creatinine drop-down select Continuous Fit > Normal and the Fitted Normal output will appear. From the Fitted Normal drop-down select Goodness of Fit. Figure 6.8 on page 86 shows the corresponding output. The p-value of <0.0001 causes a reject of the null hypothesis that the data is normally distributed. Hence, the normality assumption is not satisfied for the one-sample t-test and an alternative should be sought.

Often in colloquial use, the word "average" implies a measure of centrality for a distribution rather than the sample mean. In a skewed distribution, the median is often a better measure of centrality. The JMP Distribution > Test Mean feature offers a non-parametric alternative to the one-sample t-test, the Wilcoxon Signed Rank, which tests the median against a hypothesized value. The Wilcoxon Signed Rank test requires the data to be symmetrically distributed, which is not the case with Creatinine, so this test is not appropriate.

The column "Creatinine > 2" allows us to estimate the proportion of patients that have creatinine levels greater than 2. From Figure 6.5 on page 83, we find this proportion to be 0.637. In a sample from a distribution with a median creatinine level of 2, we would expect the proportion having a creatinine greater than two to be 0.50. A hypothesis test for a proportion can be used to determine if our proportion of 0.637 is significantly greater than 0.50. If this is the case, then we can conclude that the median creatinine is significantly larger than two.

To conduct this test of proportion, select Analyze > Distribution and enter the column "Creatinine > 2" in the Y, Columns field and click Ok. In the resulting dialog, select "Test Probabilities" from the "Creatinine > 2" drop-down window as shown in Figure 6.9 on page 87.

Figure 6.9   *Completed Dialog for Creatinine > 2 Test of Proportion*

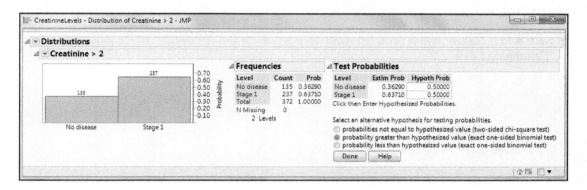

Click Done to obtain the results shown in Figure 6.10 on page 87.

Figure 6.10   *JMP Output for Test of Proportion*

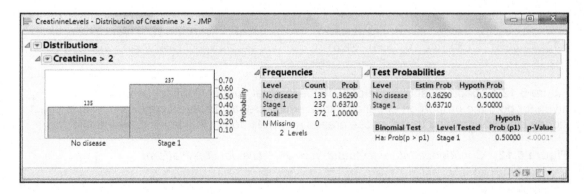

The p-value of <0.0001 is well below the 5% significance level. Hence the null hypothesis that the proportion of patients with creatinine level greater than two is 0.50 is rejected in favor of the alternative that the proportion is greater than 0.50. We conclude that the median creatinine level is significantly greater than two.

Research Question 2: What proportion of patients have creatinine levels greater than 2 mg/dL?

The point estimate for the proportion of patients that have a creatinine level greater than 2 (Stage 1 kidney insufficiency) is found in Figure 6.5 on page 83 to be 0.637. Calculating a confidence interval for the proportion will provide an interval estimate which takes into account the precision with which the proportion was estimated. Figure 6.11 on page 88 shows how to request a 95% confidence interval from the Distribution platform.

Figure 6.11 *Calculating a 95% Confidence Interval for the Proportion of Patients with Creatinine Level > 2*

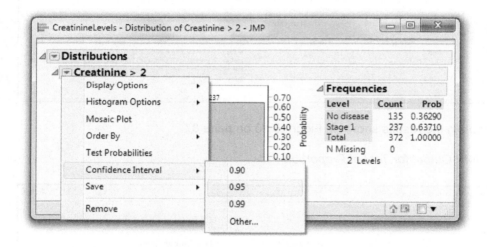

Figure 6.12 on page 88 shows the confidence interval output. Confidence intervals are given for both the proportion of patients that exhibit creatinine levels consistent with Stage 1 kidney insufficiency and those whose creatinine levels do not indicate kidney insufficiency.

Figure 6.12 *Confidence Interval Output from JMP Distribution Platform*

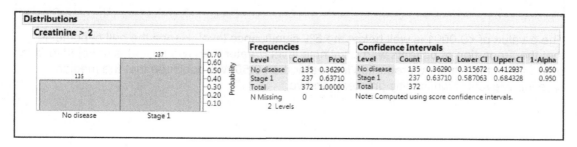

The 95% confidence interval for the proportion of patients with Creatinine > 2 (Stage 1 kidney insufficiency) is [0.587, 0.684]. This is a range of plausible values for the true proportion.

Analysis Implications

The analysis of creatinine level given in this case shows a situation where a serious violation of a one-sample t-test assumption occurred causing a need for an alternative method. This emphasizes the importance of testing assumptions. This case also illustrated the importance of visualizing each variable as a necessary first step prior to applying a statistical method. This revealed the left-skewed creatinine distribution. Not only was the one sample t-test inappropriate in this situation, but the median was a better measure of centrality than the mean due to the left-skewed creatinine distribution. While both the one sample t-test and the test of proportion shown here produced the same conclusion, in other circumstances, two different tests may lead to contradictory conclusions.

For this data, it is estimated that 63.7% of patients have creatinine levels indicative of Stage 1 kidney insufficiency. The 95% confidence interval tells us that the true proportion could be as low as 58.7% and as high as 68.4%. This suggests that the hospital should be prepared to handle patients with kidney insufficiency.

Bear in mind that the data was simulated and it is not known the extent to which it represents real patient data on kidney insufficiency. It is always prudent to review results with subject matter experts who can lend valuable insight into the interpretation of the analysis in the problem context. The data set provides additional information on other diagnoses such as diabetes and coronary artery disease. As a next step, relationships between these co-morbidities and kidney function should be examined.

Data Definitions

Column Name	Definition
patient_id	A unique number assigned to each patient
Age	Patient age in years
Race_Cat	Racial category: 1= Caucasian, 2= African-American, 3=Asian or other

Column Name	Definition
Creatinine	A chemical waste product found in blood that occurs from the normal byproduct of muscle function. It is measured in mg/dL.
Diabetes	Diabetes diagnosed 0= No, 1 = Yes
CAD	Coronary Artery Disease diagnosed: 0=No, 1=Yes
LOS	Length of inpatient hospital stay in days
Outcome	Acute Kidney Injury diagnosed 0=No, 1 =Yes

Problems

1 The test of hypothesis presented in this case used the upper limit of the Stage 1 kidney insufficiency range. Repeat the analysis this time using the lower limit of the Stage 1 range (1.6). Does your conclusion change? Which value do you recommend using to define Stage 1 kidney insufficiency? Explain why.

2 Given the results of the analyses presented in this case, what research questions would you recommend to pursue next to further understand AKI among these hospitalized patients? What statistical methods would you use to address these research questions?

3 Analyze the length of stay variable in the creatinine data set.

   a Create a histogram for this variable and choose an appropriate measure of centrality for the length of stay distribution.

   b Select a hypothesized value and an associated test of hypothesis. Conduct the test and verify that the test assumptions are satisfied.

   c Summarize your results in a few sentences.

Reference

Observational Cohort Event Analysis and Notification System (OCEANS), http://dx.doi.org/10.15147/J2VC76, accessed January 20, 2017.

7

Acute Kidney Injury in Hospitalized Patients

Chapter Summary Concepts

Statistical Concepts	Data Management Concepts	JMP Features
Descriptive statistics	Documenting data fields	Column Notes
Data visualization • Histogram • Boxplot • Normal quantile plot • Scatterplot	Reproducible research	Tabulate
Test of hypothesis		Dynamic data linking
Outlier analysis		
Logistic regression		
Odds and odds ratio		
Causality		

Background

Acute Kidney Injury (AKI) is a sudden decrease in kidney function within a few hours or days. AKI is common in hospitalized patients, especially the elderly and those in intensive care. It causes a build-up of waste products in the blood, makes it difficult for the kidneys to maintain the body's fluid balance, and can damage other organs such as the brain, heart, and lungs.

Creatinine is produced continuously by the normal breakdown of muscle tissues. Kidneys filter creatinine which is excreted into urine. Blood tests for creatinine measure kidney function with high levels indicating poor kidney function. The normal range for creatinine is 0.84 to 1.21 milligrams per deciliter (mg/dL), but this can vary based on gender and age. Creatinine levels can temporarily be elevated due to dehydration, recent red meat consumption, and certain medications. Creatinine levels from 1.6 – 2.0 indicate Stage 1 kidney insufficiency (damage). In this case we examine the length of inpatient hospital stay for those patients with and without acute kidney injury.

Problem Statement

In this case, we explore the following research questions:

1 Does inpatient length of stay differ between patients with and without AKI?

2 How does the likelihood of having AKI change with length of inpatient hospital stay?

The Data

Data was obtained from the Integrating Data for Analysis, Anonymization and SHaring (iDASH) website[1] for 372 hospital patients. The data for this case is synthetic, as it is difficult to obtain open-source patient-level medical information due to privacy concerns. The file CreatinineLevels.jmp contains the creatinine levels for these patients, length of hospital stay, the presence of selected medical conditions, and demographic factors.

Data Management

In the case "Creatinine Levels in Hospitalized Patients," the data file CreatinineLevels.jmp was prepared for analysis and an indicator variable was added to identify those patients with creatinine levels greater than 2. A best practice is to document all columns in a data file either directly in the file or in a codebook. This includes both source and derived data (new variables created from source data). A properly annotated data file is a valuable reference useful throughout the data analysis and reporting process.

The JMP Notes feature allows documentation to be added to the columns in a data table. To document the addition of the column "Creatinine > 2" right click the column header and select Column Info. From the Column Properties drop-down menu select Notes. This will open a field where information can be added about this column. An example is shown in Figure 7.1 on page 96.

---

1   The iDASH repository (https://idash-data.ucsd.edu) is supported by the National Institutes of Health through the NIH Roadmap for Medical Research, Grant U54HL108460.

Figure 7.1 Adding a Note to a Column

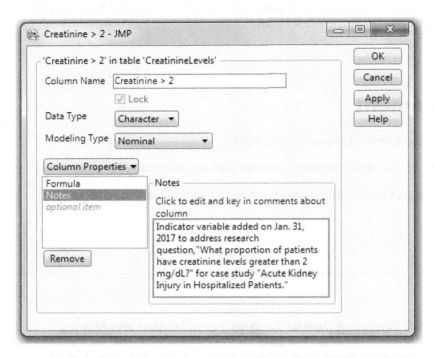

Including this type of documentation is consistent with the practice of creating reproducible research (American Statistical Association, 2017).

Analytic Approach

The problem statement poses two research questions: "Does inpatient length of stay differ between patients with and without AKI?" and "How does the likelihood of having AKI change with length of stay?" The three questions below will guide the selection of appropriate statistical methods.

1 What is the response (Y) of interest and how is it measured? For the first research question, the length of stay is of interest. It is a continuous variable. For the second research question the outcome variable is a diagnosis of AKI, which is a nominal variable.

2 Are predictor variables mentioned in the problem statement? If so, how many and what are their measurement levels? Outcome (absence or presence of AKI) is in the role of predictor in the first research question. Lengthy of stay takes on the role of predictor in the second research question.

3 What are you being asked to deliver? A data description, an interval estimate, an answer to a question, or a predictive model? For the first research question, a test of hypothesis is appropriate to determine if statistically significant difference in length of stay exists based on the presence of AKI. For the second research question, a statistical model that describes the relationship between the likelihood of AKI and length of hospital stay will address the research question.

JMP Analysis

Descriptive Analysis

In the case "Creatinine Levels in Hospitalized Patients" we visualized each variable in the data set individually using the JMP Distribution platform as shown in Figure 6.5. The average length of stay for these patients is 14.1 days with a minimum of 0 and a maximum of 29. Of the 372 patients, 25% have acute kidney injury. The problem statement asks us to consider inpatient length of stay. Patients having a length of stay of 0 would have been treated at the hospital on an outpatient basis; their records should not be included in this analysis. Select those rows with LOS = 0 using the JMP data filter. Select Rows > Data Filter, highlight LOS and click Add. Drag the right hand slider to 0. The completed Data Filter dialog is shown in Figure 7.2 on page 97.

Figure 7.2   *Completed Data Filter Dialog to Select Rows Where LOS=0*

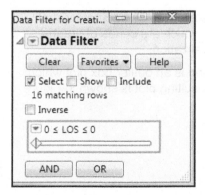

The rows where LOS=0 will be highlighted in the data table. Right-click over one of the highlighted rows and select the Exclude and Hide option. This will exclude these observations from subsequent analyses and hide them in subsequent graphs.

Since this is a comparative analysis, it is beneficial to describe the data separately for each group, those with AKI and those without AKI. JMP Graph Builder can easily create two length of stay histograms, one for those patients with AKI and one for those patients without AKI.

Drag LOS into the X drop zone and Outcome into the Y Group drop zone. Select the histogram icon from the Control Panel. The resulting data visualization is shown in Figure 7.3 on page 98.

Figure 7.3 *Histograms of Length of Stay by Outcome*

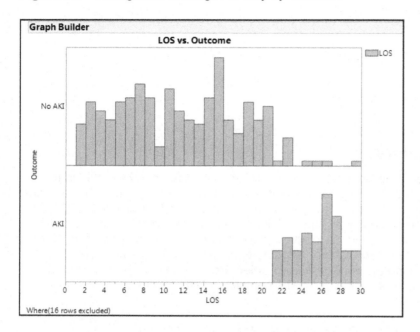

Notice that the resulting chart includes the count of excluded rows.

Graph Builder uses the same axis scales for both histograms allowing an accurate visual comparison. This is an example of the use of small multiples, which are series of graphs plotted on the same scale. This is a best practice in data visualization.

An alternate data visualization that facilities outlier identification is an outlier box plot which can be selected from the Graph Builder Control Panel. The resulting plot is shown in Figure 7.4 on page 99.

Figure 7.4   *Outlier Box Plots for Length of Stay by Outcome*

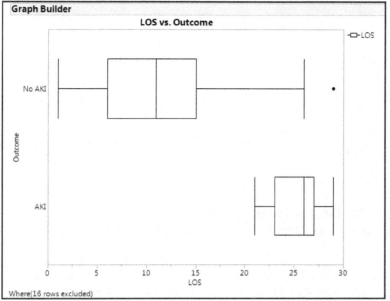

The box indicates the middle 50% of the data (the first quartile to the third quartile). The first quartile corresponds the 25th percentile, where 25% of the length of stays are below that value. For the AKI group, the 25th percentile is 23 days. The vertical line inside the box is the median. The "whiskers" are the first quartile minus 1.5 times the interquartile range (third quartile – first quartile) and the third quartile plus 1.5 times the interquartile range. Outliers are indicated as dots that lie beyond the end of the whiskers. Box plots are a compact way to visualize a data distribution including its center, spread, skewness, and outliers.

In the No AKI box plot we observe an outlier with a length of stay of 29 days. Click on the dot to highlight the corresponding patient record in the JMP data table. This is an example of JMP's dynamic data linking feature, where an observation or group of observations highlighted in either a data table or graph will be highlighted in all other data tables and graphs. The highlighted record is for Patient_ID = 7581, a 92 year old African-American man with no co-morbidities. Further investigation should be conducted with the help of a subject matter expert to determine if this outlier should be removed from the data set. Outliers are removed, not based on their influence on the statistical results, but on an understanding of the data in the domain context, and should be dispositioned accordingly. For example, if investigation revealed a data collection or recording error, then either a corrected value should be entered or the observation removed. Exclusion of observations should be documented in accordance with the practices of reproducible research.

Finally, Figure 7.5 on page 100 shows a table of descriptive statistics for length of stay by outcome. This can be accomplished using Tabulate where LOS and the desired statistics are placed in the drop zone for Rows and the nominal variable Outcome is placed into the drop zone for Columns.

Figure 7.5 *Descriptive Statistics for Length of Stay by Outcome*

Tabulate

		Outcome	
		AKI	**No AKI**
LOS	N	93	263
	% of Total	44.7%	55.3%
	Mean	25.2	11.0
	Median	26	11
	Std Dev	2.3	6.1
	Min	21	1
	Max	29	29

16 rows have been excluded.

Research Question 1: Does length of stay differ between patients with and without AKI?

This research question can be answered by conducting a two-independent samples t-test that will determine if the mean length of stay for the AKI group differs from that of the group without AKI. The two-independent samples t-test is an appropriate statistical method to apply when the dependent variable is continuous and the independent variable is nominal with two levels. This test assumes that the lengths of stay for both groups are normally distributed. The Normal quantile plots for these two groups do not show serious departures from normality. In the problems at the end of this case, you will be asked to create and assess these plots.

To begin, select Analyze > Fit Y by X and enter LOS into the Y field and Outcome into the X field. There are two different two-independent samples t-test available in JMP. The test to apply depends on whether the length of stay variances of the two groups (AKI and No AKI) are equal or unequal. Several equality of variance tests are available from the Fit Y by X drop-down menu option Unequal Variances. The JMP output is shown in Figure 7.6 on page 101.

Figure 7.6 *Equality of Variance Tests*

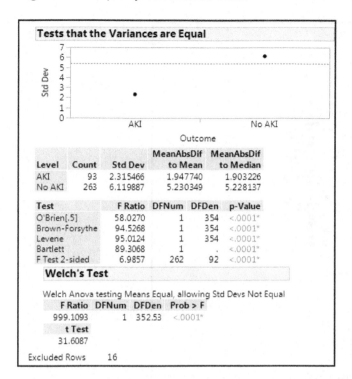

Tests that the Variances are Equal

Level	Count	Std Dev	MeanAbsDif to Mean	MeanAbsDif to Median
AKI	93	2.315466	1.947740	1.903226
No AKI	263	6.119887	5.230349	5.228137

Test	F Ratio	DFNum	DFDen	p-Value
O'Brien[.5]	58.0270	1	354	<.0001*
Brown-Forsythe	94.5268	1	354	<.0001*
Levene	95.0124	1	354	<.0001*
Bartlett	89.3068	1	.	<.0001*
F Test 2-sided	6.9857	262	92	<.0001*

Welch's Test

Welch Anova testing Means Equal, allowing Std Devs Not Equal

F Ratio	DFNum	DFDen	Prob > F
999.1093	1	352.53	<.0001*

t Test
31.6087

Excluded Rows   16

The Levene test is a good general equality of variance test. The null hypothesis is that the variances of the two groups are equal versus the alternative that they are not equal. Small p-values (less than 0.05) cause the null hypothesis to be rejected. For this data, the Levene test p-value is <0.0001 which is significant at the 5% level, so the variance of the length of stay for the AKI group is significantly different from the group without AKI.

Now we are ready to perform the t-test. When the variances are not equal, the option to select from the Fit Y by X drop-down menu is t Test. The null hypothesis for the two sample t-test is that the means of the two groups are equal with an alternative that the means are not equal. The results for the length of stay data are shown in Figure 7.7 on page 102.

Figure 7.7 *Two-independent sample t-test for Unequal Variances*

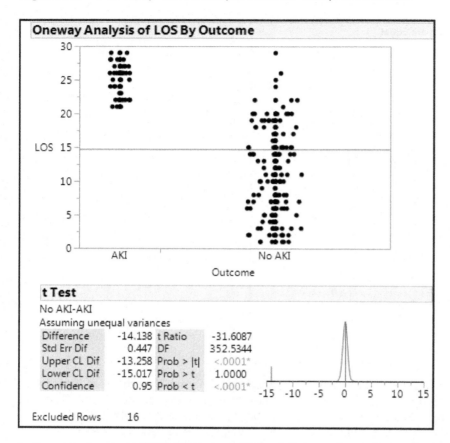

In the plot showing LOS by Outcome, the points have been "jittered" which spreads out the markers to avoid overplotting and gives you a better sense of the data density (From the Oneway Analysis of LOS by Outcome drop-down, select Display Options > Points Jittered).

The length of stay for patients without AKI is on average 14.1 days lower than for patients with AKI. Is this difference statistically significant? The null hypothesis for the t-test is that the length of stay means of the two patient groups (with and without AKI) are equal. The p-value associated with the t-test determines if the observed difference (-14.1) is statistically significant. P-values less than the chosen significance level indicate that the two patient groups are on average significantly different. The JMP output for the t-test gives three possible p-values, two associated with the one-sided alternatives (greater than and less than) and one associated with the two-sided alternative (not equal). The correct p-value depends on how the alternative hypothesis was specified and is derived from the research question. For this research question we want to see if there is a difference between the two patient groups which corresponds to a two-sided ($\neq$) alternative. The correct p-value is Prob > |t| <0.0001 as shown in Figure 7.7 on page 102, which indicates a statistically significant difference at the 5% level. This means that on average patients without AKI have length of stay 14.1 days shorter than patients with AKI.

Research Question 2: How does the likelihood of having AKI change with length of stay?

A statistical model quantifying the relationship between length of stay and AKI diagnosis will address this research question. When the dependent variable (Outcome) is nominal and there is a continuous independent variable (LOS), a logistic regression will yield such a statistical model. A logistic regression expresses the natural log odds of the dependent variable as a linear function of the independent variable. Odds expresses the likelihood of an event occurring and is calculated as the ratio of the number of occurrences of the event to the number of times the event did not occur. For this data, the odds of having AKI are 93/263 = 0.354; the odds of not having AKI for hospitalized patients is 263/93 = 2.828. This means that a hospitalized patient is almost three times more likely to not have AKI than to have AKI. It is easier to understand the likelihood when expressed in the form that is greater than one. Odds can be expressed in terms of probability as p/(1-p). The probability of having AKI, p, is 93/356 = 0.261.

A logistic regression equation can be estimated with the Fit Y by X platform by entering Outcome in the Y field and LOS in the X field. The JMP output is shown in Figure 7.8 on page 104.

Figure 7.8 JMP Logistic Regression Output

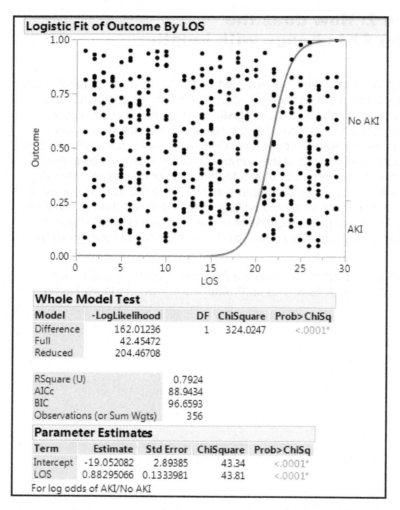

The Whole Model Test uses a Chi-square test to determine whether the logistic regression model is significant in explaining the relationship between the likelihood of AKI and length of stay. In this case, the Chi-square test yields a p-value of <0.0001 which is significant at the 5% level.

The fitted logistic regression coefficients are given in the Parameter Estimates table. The logistic regression equation relating LOS and log odds of having AKI to not having AKI is:

ln odds(AKI/No AKI) = −19.052 + 0.883*LOS

This is the estimated log odds ratio of having AKI to not having AKI for a given length of stay. A chi-square test is used to determine if the regression coefficient for LOS is significantly different from zero. For this data, LOS is a significant predictor of AKI (p<0.0001) at the 5% significance level. The plot in Figure 7.8 on page 104 shows the logistic regression model as a blue curve. Notice that the y-axis scale is in terms of the probability, not odds.

It is not intuitive to think in terms of a log odds ratio. Exponentiating the regression coefficient for LOS gives what is referred to as the unit odds ratio which is the odds ratio associated with a one-unit increase in the LOS.

The odds ratio can be obtained from the drop-down menu associated Logistic Fit Outcome by LOS as shown in Figure 7.9 on page 105.

Figure 7.9 *Obtaining Odds Ratio Output for Logistic Regression*

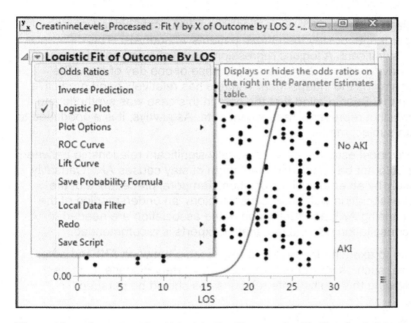

The odds ratio output is added to the Parameter Estimates table as shown in Figure 7.10 on page 105.

Figure 7.10 *Odds Ratio Output for Logistic Regression*

Logistic Fit of Outcome By LOS

Parameter Estimates

Term	Estimate	Std Error	ChiSquare	Prob>ChiSq	Unit Odds Ratio	Odds Ratio
Intercept	-19.052082	2.89385	43.34	<.0001*	.	.
LOS	0.88295066	0.1333981	43.81	<.0001*	2.41802396	5.4563e+10

For log odds of AKI/No AKI

The odds ratio of AKI to No AKI associated with an increase in one day of length of stay is 2.42.

RSquare (U) gives a measure of goodness-of-fit on a scale of 0 to 1. An RSquare (U) of 0 indicates that the model does not predict the outcome (AKI) and an RSquare (U) of 1 indicates that the logistic regression model is a perfect predictor of the outcome (AKI). For this data the Rsquare (U) is 0.7924 indicating relatively good predictability.

Analysis Implications

In a sample of 356 hospitalized patients, 25% were diagnosed with acute kidney injury and had on average a 14.1 longer length of stay than those patients without AKI. This difference was found to be statistically significant. A logistic regression model showed an odds ratio (odds of AKI to odds of not having AKI) of 2.418 for an increase of one day of stay. The logistic model with length of stay as the independent variable has relatively good predictive capability for acute kidney injury. Bear in mind that the data in this case was synthetic and it is not known the extent to which it represents real patient data. As always, it is a good idea to review statistical results with subject matter experts.

While the logistic regression model established a statistically significant relationship between AKI and length of stay, it should not be concluded that length of stay causes AKI. Causality cannot be substantiated solely by an empirical association. Temporal precedence of the causal factor, elimination of association with other causal factors, an understanding of the physiological mechanisms causing AKI, and replication of the association are needed to establish causality. Again, consultation with subject matter experts is recommended.

Next analysis steps would be to examine the bivariate relationship between AKI and other variables given in the data set such as co-morbidities (coronary artery disease, diabetes), age, and length of stay. Following this multivariate relationships should be pursued.

Table 7.1 *Data Definitions*

Column Name	Definition
patient_id	A unique patient identifier
Age	Patient age in years
Race_Cat	Racial category: 1= Caucasian, 2= African-American, 3=Asian or other
Creatinine	A chemical waste product found in blood that occurs from the normal byproduct of muscle function. It is measured in mg/dL.
Diabetes	Diabetes diagnosed: No, Yes

Column Name	Definition
CAD	Coronary Artery Disease diagnosed: No, Yes
LOS	Length of inpatient hospital stay in days
Outcome	Acute Kidney Injury diagnosed: No, Yes
Creatinine > 2	Indicates if patient creatinine level is greater than 2 or not

Problems

1 Construct Normal Quantile plots for length of stay by outcome. Do you think the normality assumptions is satisfied for both groups? Explain why or why not.

2 What is the appropriate statistical method to determine if there is an association between a diagnosis of AKI and a diagnosis of coronary artery disease? Conduct this analysis in JMP and interpret the results.

3 Create a visualization of the distribution of length of stay by racial category (Race_cat) and AKI diagnosis (Outcome). (Hint: Replicate the charts shown in Figure 7.3 on page 98 and Figure 7.4 on page 99 and then drag Race_cat into the Group X drop zone.) Discuss the differences in the distributions of racial category.

4 Discuss what additional patient medical information would be helpful in achieving an improved understanding of AKI?

References

Observational Cohort Event Analysis and Notification System (OCEANS), http://dx.doi.org/10.15147/J2VC76, accessed January 20, 2017.

"Recommendations to Funding Agencies for Supporting Reproducible Research," American Statistical Association, January 17, 2017, accessed February 4, 2017 at https://www.amstat.org/asa/files/pdfs/POL-ReproducibleResearchRecommendations.pdf

8

Visualizing Influenza Activity

Chapter Summary Concepts

Statistical Concepts	Data Management Concepts	JMP Features
Visualizing time dependent data	Extracting a subset of data	Graph Builder

Statistical Concepts	Data Management Concepts	JMP Features
Data Visualization		Tables > Subset
• Bar chart		
• Histogram		
• Box plot		
• Line graph		
		Data Filter
		Annotate

Background

Influenza (commonly called the flu) is a contagious respiratory illness caused by viruses. The flu usually comes on suddenly with symptoms including fever, sore throat, runny or stuffy nose, muscle or body aches, headaches, and fatigue. Most people who get influenza recover in several days to less than two weeks. Young children, older adults, pregnant women, and those with certain chronic medical conditions are at high risk of serious flu complications, possibly requiring hospitalization and sometimes resulting in death.

There are three types of influenza viruses: A, B and C. Influenza A and B cause seasonal epidemics almost every winter in the United States. Influenza C infections cause a mild respiratory illness and are not thought to cause epidemics.

While seasonal influenza viruses can be detected year-round in the United States, they are most common during the fall and winter. The exact timing and duration of flu seasons can vary, but activity often begins to increase in October. Most of the time flu activity peaks between December and March, and can last into May.

States report a variety of measures to the CDC for each week in the flu season (October to May) including:

■ The numbers of each type of the influenza virus identified by public health laboratories

■ The percentage of their populations experiencing influenza-like illness

■ The geographic spread of flu activity within their borders – widespread, regional, or sporadic

■ The number of influenza-associated hospitalizations

- The number of influenza-associated deaths
- The number of respiratory specimens testing positive for influenza
- The numbers of each type of influenza affecting each age group

Flu outbreaks can affect the operation of many organizations and a variety of decisions need to be made before and during the flu season to compensate for absenteeism and limit disease spread. Long-term care facilities and hospitals must determine if visiting policies should be modified. Health care providers need to schedule patients for vaccinations and obtain sufficient inventories of medications and supplies to treat flu sufferers. Schools experiencing severe outbreaks may choose to close. Local, state, and national public health organizations monitor flu activity and prepare awareness campaigns to encourage vaccination and proper hygiene. Advance planning decisions can be informed by an understanding of the year-to-year variation in flu activity, while decisions made during the flu season may benefit from monitoring weekly activity. In this case we will make use of Graph Builder to construct visualizations of flu activity on an annual and weekly basis for two states.

Problem Statement

Compare the flu activity between two states, one located on the east coast (New York) and one located in the center of the United States (Missouri). Prepare data visualizations that will address the following questions:

1 How does historical flu activity compare between New York and Missouri over seven flu seasons (2009-2010 to 2015-2016)?

2 How does flu activity compare between New York and Missouri on a weekly basis for the most recently completed flu season (2015-2016)?

The Data

Weekly flu activity data was obtained from the Department of Health websites for New York and Missouri for the 33 or 34 weeks of the seven flu seasons from 2009-2010 to 2015-2016. The number of reported laboratory confirmed cases of flu types A, B, and Not Specified and the total number of influenza cases are included in the file flu_NY_MO.jmp by week for the seven flu seasons for each of the two states.

Data Management

Create a new JMP data table with the only the 2015-2016 season weekly data by selecting Rows > Data Filter, choose the Season column. Pick the 2015-2016 season (66 rows will be selected). This will highlight the rows associated with the 2015-1016 season. To create a new data table from these rows, select Tables > Subset. Assign a new file name to this data table.

Analytic Approach

The problem statement asks us to create visualizations to compare flu activity between New York and Missouri. The three questions below will guide the selection of appropriate methods.

1 What is the response (Y) of interest and how is it measured? The response variable is the total number of flu cases, which is a continuous variable.

2 Are predictor variables mentioned in the problem statement? If so, how many and what are their measurement levels? The research questions mention state and date as variables by which flu activity should be visualized. State is a nominal variable and date is a continuous variable.

3 What are you being asked to deliver? A data description, an interval estimate, an answer to a question, or a predictive model? You are being asked to provide a descriptive summary of flu activity. Visualization is an effective way to display time dependent data. For the first research question, we are comparing the total number of flu cases reported by state and season. For the second research question, we are displaying weekly data for a single flu season for each state.

JMP Analysis

Comparing States over Multiple Flu Seasons

We begin by examining the variation in the total number of flu cases reported each season for New York and Missouri. JMP's Graph Builder is a flexible platform that allows many different types of graphs to be created.

Open flu_NY_MO.jmp and invoke Graph > Graph Builder from the JMP Menu. Drag the variable, Total Influenza to the Y drop zone, Season to the X drop zone, and State to the Group Y drop zone. Choose the Bar chart icon in the control panel and select Sum from the Summary Statistic drop-down menu. The completed Graph Builder dialog is shown in Figure 8.1 on page 113.

Figure 8.1   *Graph Builder Dialog to Create Bar Charts of Total Influenza Cases by State*

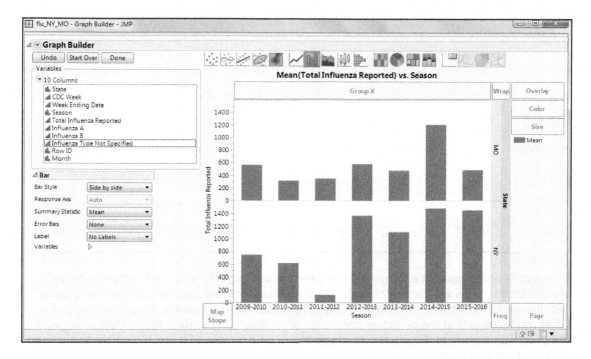

This visualization shows the total number of flu cases reported in each season by state. Notice that the Y-axis is automatically scaled to the same range for both bar charts. This facilitates comparison between the two states.

Showing More Detail for Each Flu Season

The flu activity data is given weekly for each of the seven seasons. In the bar charts of Figure 8.1 on page 113 the Summary Statistic chosen was Sum. This aggregated the total cases for a season across all weeks. A more detailed comparison of the flu seasons can be made by looking at the distributions of weekly flu activity. Histograms are commonly used to display data distributions. With the Graph Builder dialog set as in Figure 8.1 on page 113, choose the Histogram icon from the control panel. Figure 8.2 on page 114 shows the resulting graph.

Figure 8.2 *Histograms of Weekly Influenza Cases by Season and State*

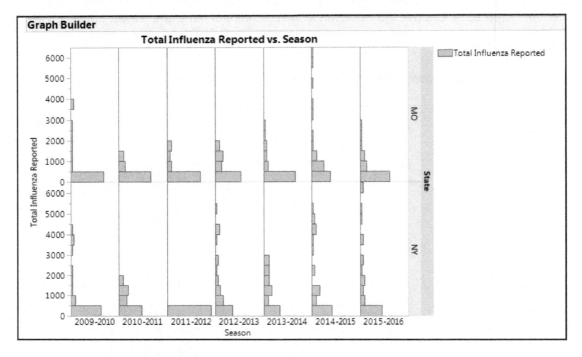

This matrix of histograms exemplifies the data visualization technique of "small multiples" popularized by Edward Tufte. This method of multivariate data display uses similar graphs with the same axis scales sequenced over one or two other variables. The advantage of small multiples is that the observer can focus on changes in the data rather than changes in the graphical elements. Figure 8.2 on page 114 is an example of a small multiple sequenced over Season and State.

Unfortunately, the skewness of the weekly flu activity coupled with the display of 14 histograms makes it difficult to discern differences across either seasons or states. Box plots are an alternative way to visualize data distributions. In a box plot, a data distribution is summarized by a box whose ends lie at the 25th and 75th percentiles. The line inside the box shows the median. The "whiskers" extend (1.5*Interquartile range) beyond the ends of the box. Outliers beyond the whiskers are shown as dots. While box plots have less detail about the distributional shape than histograms, they are effective when comparing a relatively large number of groups in a small space. To create a matrix of box plots, select the box plot icon from the Graph Builder control panel. The result is shown in Figure 8.3 on page 115.

Figure 8.3 *Box Plots of Weekly Influenza Cases by Season and State*

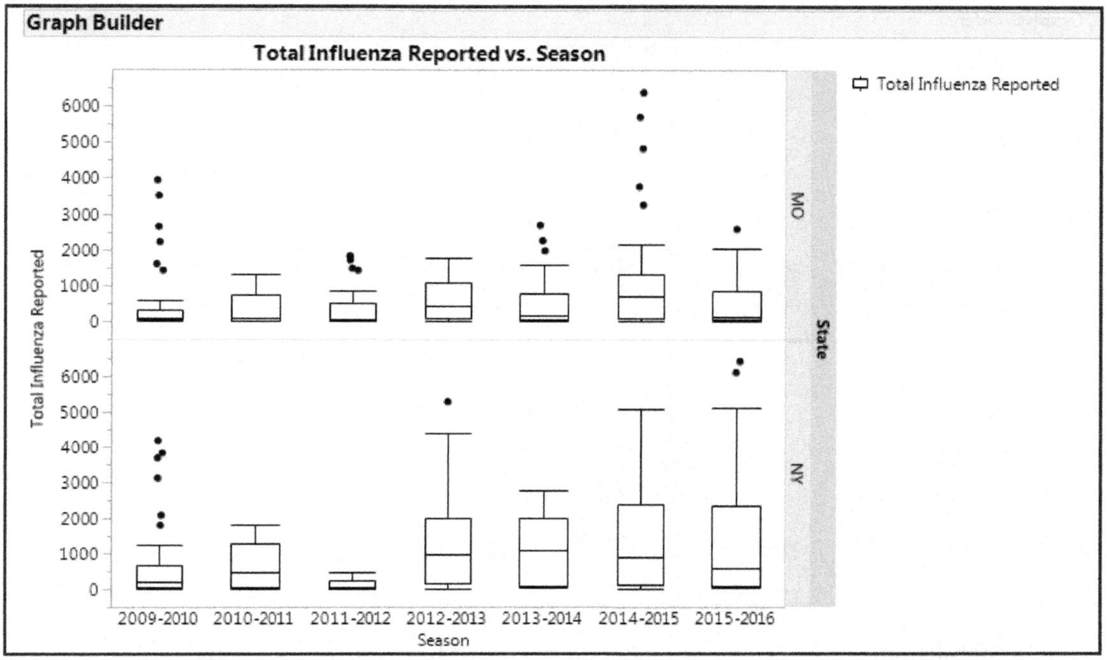

This visualization is more effective for comparing the weekly distributions of flu activity than the histograms shown in Figure 8.2 on page 114. The choice of graph type (e.g., box plot, histogram) that is most effective will depend on the data distributions and the number of small multiples to be displayed. Graph Builder's control panel makes it easy to evaluate different graphs.

Annotating Graphs

Data visualizations can be improved by judiciously annotating graphs with problem domain information. During the seven seasons being analyzed, the H1N1 pandemic occurred in the 2009-2010 flu season and in 2012 the FDA approved the use of cell-based technology for manufacturing flu vaccine. This new technology allows vaccines to be produced more rapidly than the traditional egg-based manufacturing process.

The JMP Annotate tool allows text boxes to be added to graphs. Figure 8.4 on page 116 shows the bar charts for total influenza cases with the addition of two text boxes.

Figure 8.4 *Total Influenza Cases Bar Charts with Annotations Added*

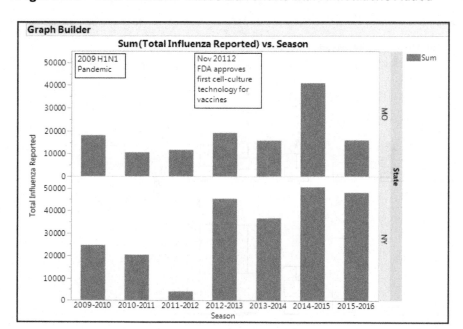

When annotating graphs, place text boxes on charts so that they do not obscure the graphical elements. Avoid excessive annotation, which will detract from the effectiveness of the graph. Annotations provide additional information that improves the interpretation of the data in the context of the problem domain.

Figure 8.4 on page 116 allows us to easily compare the Missouri and New York flu activity by season. Both states experienced the highest level of flu activity during the 2014-2015 season. New York's flu activity remained relatively high from 2012-2013 to 2015-2016 while Missouri only experienced the high level in 2014-2015. Both states saw relatively low flu activity during the 2009 pandemic.

Comparing States by Week for the 2015-2016 Flu Season

During a flu season, activity can be monitored on a weekly basis. Again, Graph Builder offers a flexible platform for data visualization. In order to look at the 2015-2016 season for changes week-to-week, open the 2015-2016 flu season JMP file, created in the Data Management section. This contains weekly data for both New York and Missouri for the 2015-2016 flu season.

Select Graph Builder from the JMP menu. Drag Total Influenza to the Y drop zone. Drag Week Ending Date to the X drop zone. Notice that the dates are placed in chronological order along the axis. In the control panel select the line icon. Drag State to both the Overlay and Color drop zones. The completed Graph Builder dialog is shown in Figure 8.5 on page 117.

Figure 8.5 *Graph Builder Dialog to Create Line Graphs for Weekly Flu Activity for the 2015-2016 Season*

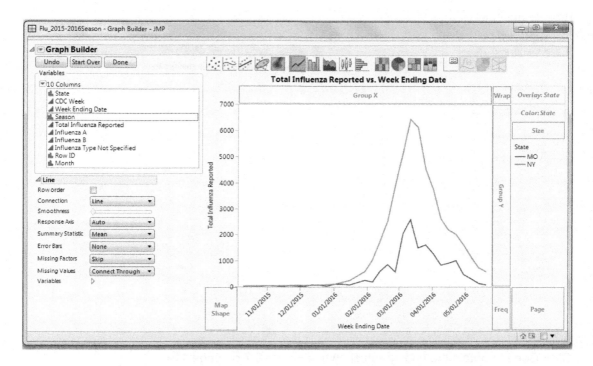

Each state's weekly flu activity is displayed as a separate line graph on the same X and Y axes. Place the cursor anywhere over one of the lines and right click. Click Add > Points to add markers to the line graphs as shown in Figure 8.6 on page 118.

Figure 8.6 Graph Builder Dialog to Add Markers

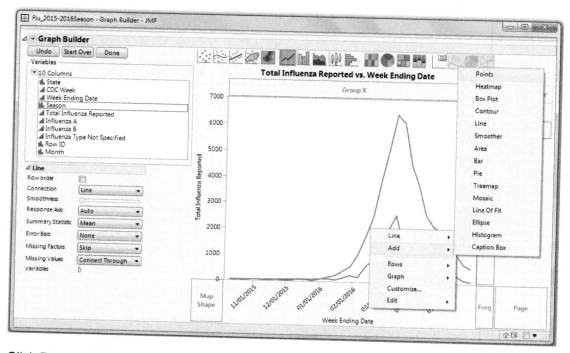

Click Done to obtain the final graph shown in Figure 8.7 on page 119.

Figure 8.7   *Line Graphs of Weekly Influenza Cases by State*

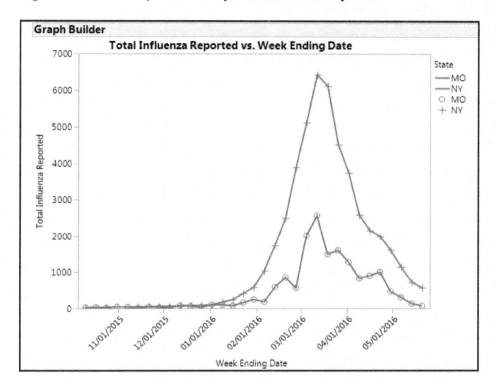

Different markers enable the lines corresponding to each state to be distinguished when the graph is reproduced in black-and-white.

When there are multiple line graphs displayed on a single set of axes, the lines may be difficult to distinguish. In these cases, creating a small multiple display may be preferable. This can be accomplished in Graph Builder by dragging State from the Overlay drop zone to the Y groups drop zone. The result is shown in Figure 8.8 on page 120.

Figure 8.8 *Line (Smooth) Graph for New York and Missouri for the Weeks of the 2015-2016 Flu Season, with Overlay by Color*

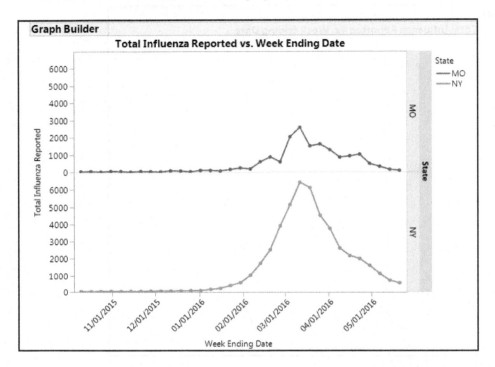

Both Figure 8.7 on page 119 and Figure 8.8 on page 120 show that at the peak of the flu season, New York has more cases reported than Missouri. This is to be expected as New York has a larger population than Missouri. For both states flu peaks at roughly the same time (early March).

Finally, we create a small multiple display that shows the pattern of flu activity for the two states for flu types A and B. In Graph Builder drag Influenza A to the Y drop zone then drag Influenza B to the Y drop zone. This will create two Y axes, one for each flu type. Drag State to the X group drop zone and Week Ending Date into the X drop zone. Select the line icon from the control panel and add markers as described above. The resulting graph is shown in Figure 8.9 on page 121.

Figure 8.9 *Small Multiple Display of Weekly Flu Activity by State and Flu Type for the 2015-2016 Season*

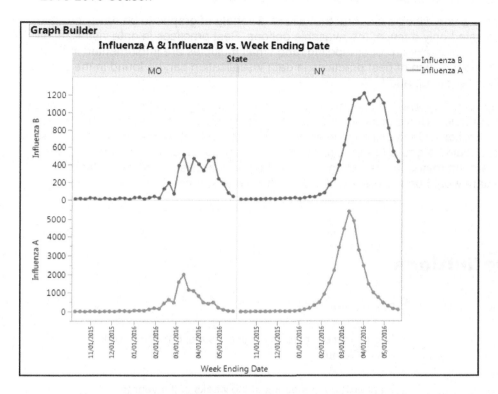

In this display, we see the differences between the two strains of flu with the peaks occurring at the same time but lasting longer for Influenza B. This pattern was consistent between both states.

Analysis Implications

Analyzing time dependent data visually is a quick and effective way to identify patterns and make comparisons. The Centers for Disease Control publishes a weekly surveillance report during the flu season that contains a number of graphical displays including bar charts and line graphs. In this form, flu information is easily understood by both the general public and health care professionals. Many states also publish weekly flu surveillance reports through their websites.

The data plotted in this case is the number of reported cases in each state and we are limited to comparing time patterns between the two states. New York has a larger population and as such would be expected to have a higher number of seasonal flu cases. In order to compare the weekly flu incidence between the two states, these raw counts would need to be transformed to rates, such as number per 100,000 population.

Graph Builder is a very flexible platform that allows a variety of graphs to be easily created. This case illustrated only a few of the available options. Best practices in data visualization such as equally scaled axes, proper labeling, and small multiples are implemented in Graph Builder. Further discussion of best practices in data visualization can be found in the seminal works of Tufte, Cleveland, and Few.

When building data displays it is important to design them to deliver the desired message to the intended audience. Static displays such as those presented in this case are appropriate for printed publications. Such displays need to conform to publication standards, and these visualizations should be geared to the publication's target audience. In some circumstances, stakeholders are interested in interacting with the data. In that case, a dynamic dashboard to visualize the data would be more appropriate to fulfill the user's needs.

Data Definitions

Data Element	Description
State	Two character abbreviation of the state: NY = New York, MS = Missouri)
CDC Week	Standardized numbering of the weeks of the year to allow year-to-year comparison. Each CDC week begins on Sunday and ends on the following Saturday. Week 1 of the year ends on the first Saturday of January, provided that it is at least the fourth day into the month of January.
Week Ending Date	Month/Day/Year of the end of the reported week
Season	Year range of the flu season
Total Influenza Reported	Total number of laboratory confirmed flu cases reported for the week
Influenza A	Number of influenza type A cases reported for the week
Influenza B	Number of influenza type B cases reported for the week

Data Element	Description
Influenza Type Not Specified	Number of influenza type not specified cases reported for the week

Problems

1 Recreate the bar charts and line graphs shown in this case. Experiment with other types of graphs and options available through Graph Builder. Compare and contrast the graphs you created to those given in the case.

2 Choose two other states and download the flu activity data from their state Department of Health websites for the same time periods as in this case. Reproduce the graphs given in this case. Discuss similarities and differences in the flu activity for these two states.

3 Research best practices in data visualization then download a weekly flu surveillance report for either the Centers for Disease Control or a state department of health. Evaluate the data visualizations presented and identify where best practices in data visualization have been implemented and where improvements could be made.

References

Cleveland, William S., *The Elements of Graphing Data, 2nd ed.*, Hobart Press, 1994.

Few, Stephen, *Show Me the Numbers: Designing Tables and Graphs to Enlighten, 2nd ed.*, Analytics Press, 2012.

Tufte, Edward R., *The Visual Display of Quantitative Information, 2nd ed.*, Graphics Press, 2001.

9

Appointment Wait Times at Veterans Medical Centers

Chapter Summary Concepts

Statistical Concepts	Data Management Concepts	JMP Features
Data visualization	Creating derived data	Formula Editor
• Histogram		
• Needle chart		
• Point chart		
• Overlay plot		
• Bubble plot		
• Geographic map		
	Concatenating data elements	Column Information > Notes
		Reorder Columns
		Graph > Chart
		Graph > Overlay Plot
		Graph > Bubble Plot
		Graph Builder
		Maps

Background

The United States Department of Veterans Affairs (VA) is a cabinet-level agency which provides veterans with medical care and benefits in additional to administering national cemeteries. Currently, the Veterans Health Administration (VHA) operates over 1233 health care facilities including 168 medical centers and 1053 outpatient clinics. Nearly nine million veterans receive care through the VHA annually. The VHA is organized regionally into 18 Veterans Integrated Service Networks (VISN). VHA medical centers can be found in metropolitan areas and provide both in- and out-patient services such as surgery, critical care, mental health, orthopedics, and physical therapy. Some medical centers also offer more advanced care such as plastic surgery and organ transplantation.

In 2013, a Cable News Network (CNN) investigation revealed long wait times for appointments at some VHA medical centers and attributed some deaths to those delays. Subsequently, other media and government investigations found that some VHA medical facilities were not in compliance with VHA scheduling policies and procedures and that scheduling information was being altered to show better performance than was actually occurring. In August 2014, President Obama signed a $16 billion bill to build more VHA facilities and to hire more health care providers. Disciplinary actions, including the firing of the Secretary of Veterans Affairs, were taken to address mismanagement within the VA health care system. Despite these actions, the problem of long wait times for medical care at veterans' facilities continues.

In this case study we examine changes in the appointment backlogs at VHA medical centers from the Mid-Atlantic (VISN 6), Southeast (VISN 7), and Sunshine (VISN 8) Health Care Networks.

Problem Statement

Explore the information on VHA medical centers in the southeast for May 2015 and May 2016 including the backlog change over the course of a year. Of particular interest are the 31-60 day backlogs.

The Data

The Veterans Health Administration began providing patient access data bi-weekly through their website (https://www.va.gov/health/access-audit.asp). Included are pending appointments and electronic wait list summaries at the national, facility, and division levels. The Centers for Medicare and Medicaid Services report performance data on Veterans Health Administration medical centers accessible from the website https://www.cms.gov/Medicare/Quality-Initiatives-Patient-Assessment-Instruments/HospitalQualityInits/VA-Data.html. In this case we will utilize the Veterans Administration Inpatient Satisfaction Survey. The JMP file VHA_Appts.jmp was assembled manually from these various data sources. Pertinent information about the various columns was documented through JMP Notes (right click on the Column Header and select Column Properties > Notes).

Data Management

Introduction

The objective of this case is to become familiar with the VA medical center appointment backlog data and the characteristics of the various medical centers. Since there are multiple variables to explore, we will focus on multivariate data visualizations. Examining the data table we see that the hospitals are identified by either Provider ID or Hospital Name. In some cases, Hospital Name is quite long, and when plotted the axis labels will take up a disproportionate amount of space on the graph. Provider ID, while shorter, is a unique identifier that is not informative. Since the data file is relatively small, a new variable could be created manually with shortened hospital names. Another option is to create a hospital identifier that contains the city and state where the medical center is located.

Concatenating Two Columns

The data table does not have a column containing both city and state, but one can be easily created using the Formula Editor. Create a new column and invoke the Formula Editor either by double clicking the column header or right clicking the column header and selecting Column Properties >Formula. From the list of column names enter City and then select Character > Concat from the list of function groups. Enter ", " and then concatenate State. Note that function groups can be opened using the toggle to the left of the function group name. The completed function is shown in Figure 9.1 on page 129.

Figure 9.1 *Concatenating City and State Columns*

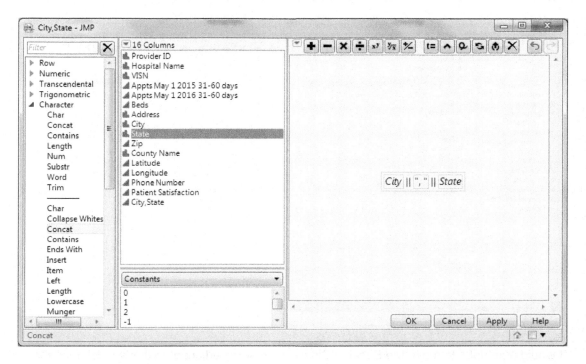

Creating a New Column

It is of interest to know if the VA medical centers are making progress towards reducing the backlog of appointments. To create the difference in the number of veterans waiting 31-60 days for an appointment, a new column should be created that subtracts the May 2015 backlog from the May 2016 backlog. Figure 9.2 on page 130 shows the formula to create the new column, Backlog Difference.

Figure 9.2 *Formula to Create the Backlog Difference*

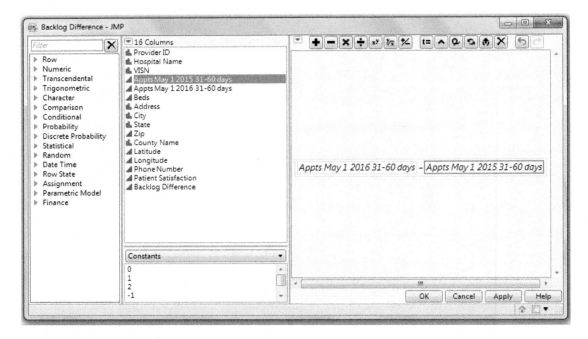

It would be helpful to move the Backlog Difference column adjacent to the two columns that show the 2015 and 2016 backlogs. Select Cols > Reorder Columns > Move Selected Column as shown in Figure 9.3 on page 130 and from the resulting Columns list move Backlog Difference after Appts May 1 2016 31-60 days.

Figure 9.3 *Reordering a JMP Column*

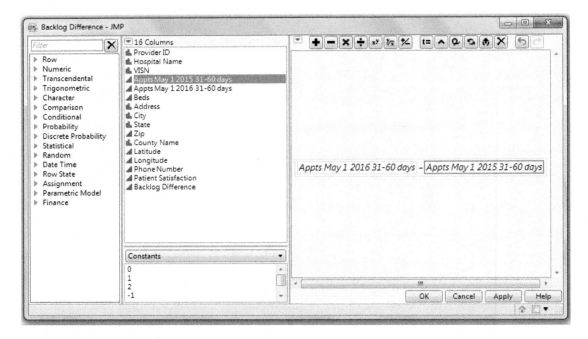

The data file is now ready for analysis.

Analytic Approach

The problem statement gives the following research questions.

- How has the backlog of veterans waiting 31-60 days for an appointment changed in a year?

- How do the VHA medical centers differ in terms of 31-60 day backlog levels, capacity (number of beds) and patient satisfaction?

The three questions below will guide the selection of appropriate statistical methods.

1 What is the response (Y) of interest and how is it measured? We are interested in exploring the variation in backlog, bed capacity, patient satisfaction, and location between the medical centers. There are both continuous and nominal variables in the data set.

2 Are predictor variables mentioned in the problem statement? If so, how many and what are their measurement levels? The problem statement specifies data exploration and does not identify any of the variables as predicted or predictor.

3 What are you being asked to deliver? A data description, an interval estimate, an answer to a question, or a predictive model? We would like to get a "picture" of the backlog performance for the VA medical centers and understand the differences between these facilities. Data visualization through univariate and multivariate graphs is an effective means to present such as picture.

JMP Analysis

Introduction

A good strategy when exploring a data set is to begin by examining each variable one at a time, then progress to bivariate and then multivariate visualizations to understand the relationships between variables.

Univariate Visualization

Visualizing the distributions of key variables is a good first step. In this case, the backlogs, bed capacity, location, and patient satisfaction scores are key variables. A histogram is a good choice to show the range of observed values and the shape of the distribution. We begin by creating histograms for the 2015 and 2016 backlogs. Select Distribution and enter

"Appts May 1 2015 31-60 days" and "Appts May 1 2016 31-60 days" in the Y field. Check the Histograms only box. The resulting histograms are shown in Figure 9.4 on page 132.

Figure 9.4 *Histograms for 2015 and 2016 Appointment Backlogs*

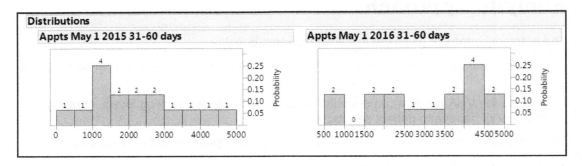

The two histograms should have the same x-axis scale to facilitate comparison. Select Uniform Scale from the Options menu next to Distributions. Figure 9.5 on page 132 shows the appointment backlogs on the same scale. Use caution when comparing the shapes of these two distributions as the histograms were created from only 16 observations.

Figure 9.5 *Histograms for 2015 and 2016 Appointment Backlogs with Uniform Scaling*

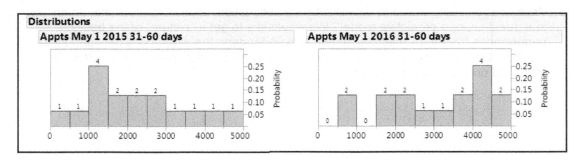

These histograms show the magnitude and variation of the backlogs.

Figure 9.6 on page 133 shows the histograms for the backlog difference, in-patient bed capacity, and the patient overall satisfaction scores.

Figure 9.6 *Histograms for Backlog Difference, Bed Capacity, and Patient Satisfaction*

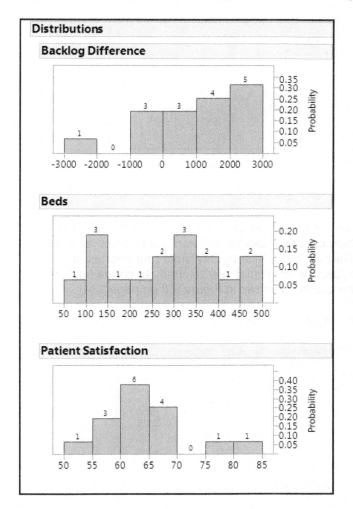

The Backlog Difference histogram shows that only four of the 16 medical centers (25%) reduced the number of veterans waiting 31-60 days for an appointment. This histogram only shows the change in the backlog, not the magnitude of the backlog. The bed capacity of these hospitals spans almost an order of magnitude. The histogram for patient satisfaction shows two of the 16 hospitals (12.5%) with relatively high ratings.

Figure 9.7 on page 134 shows the geographic distribution of the 16 medical centers by state and VISN.

Figure 9.7 *Histograms for State and VISN*

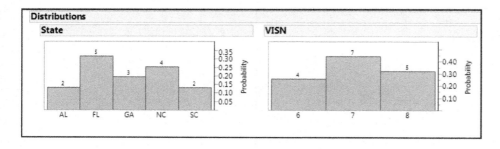

Bivariate Visualization

Since the research question focuses on the change in appointment backlogs from 2015 to 2016, we next visualize the relationships between Backlog Difference and other variables in the data set. We begin by looking at Backlog Difference by City.State (our shortened identifier for the medical center name) using a horizontal needle chart. To create this graph select Graph > Chart and complete the dialog as shown in Figure 9.8 on page 134

Figure 9.8 *Dialog to Create a Horizontal Needle Chart*

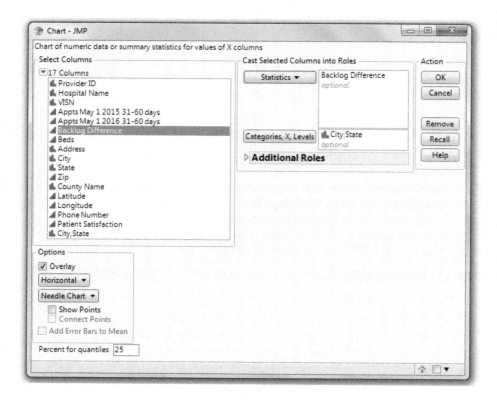

The resulting horizontal needle chart is shown in Figure 9.9 on page 135.

Figure 9.9   *Horizontal Needle Chart: Backlog Difference by City.State*

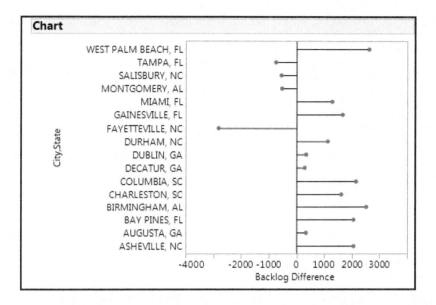

A vertical point chart is a good way to visualize the relationship between Backlog Difference and State. In the Chart dialog, highlight Backlog Difference and in the Statistics drop-down choose Data, enter State into the Categories, X, Levels field, and for the Options choose Vertical and Point Chart. The result is shown in Figure 9.10 on page 136. A reference line on the y-axis has been added by right clicking anywhere over the y-axis scale and select Axis Settings. Add the value 0 to the Reference Lines dialog. The vertical point chart is shown in Figure 9.10 on page 136.

Figure 9.10 Vertical Point Chart: Backlog Difference by State

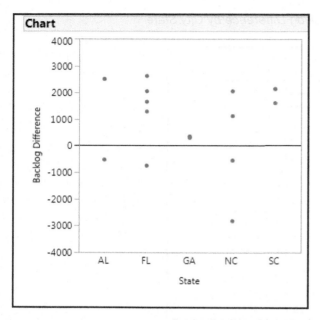

This chart shows the variability of the change in backlog by state. The Chart platform is useful for plotting a continuous variable by a nominal or ordinal variable.

Overlay graphs are appropriate for visualizing the relationship between two continuous variables. Select Graph > Overlay and enter Beds in the X field and Backlog Difference in the Y field. The X-Y plot is shown in Figure 9.11 on page 136.

Figure 9.11 Overlay Plot: Backlog Difference by Beds

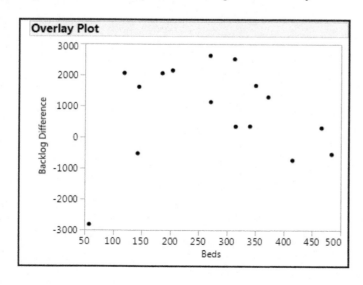

This X-Y plot shows no apparent relationship between bed capacity and backlog difference.

Other bivariate relationships can be explored using the Chart or Overlay Plot options from the Graph platform.

Multivariate Visualization: Bubble Plots

A bubble plot is an effective multivariate data visualization. Bubble plots allow up to five variables to be visualized simultaneously with variables plotted on the x- and y-axes, bubble size and color can represent two more variables, and animation allows a fifth variable to be included. Animation is useful for time dependent variables.

Bubble plots can be created from the JMP Graph menu. Figure 9.12 on page 137 shows the completed dialog needed to create a bubble plot with four variables from the VHA data table. The change in backlog is shown on the y-axis and the hospital location (city and state) appears on the x-axis. The size of the bubbles indicates the magnitude of the backlog in May 2016 and the color scale represents the size of the hospital as measured by the number of in-patient beds.

Figure 9.12   *Bubble Plot Dialog*

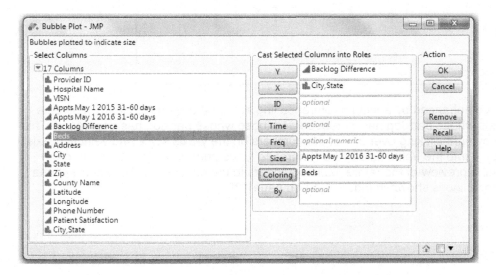

The rendered bubble plot is shown in Figure 9.13 on page 138.

Figure 9.13 Bubble Plot for VHA Appointment Backlogs

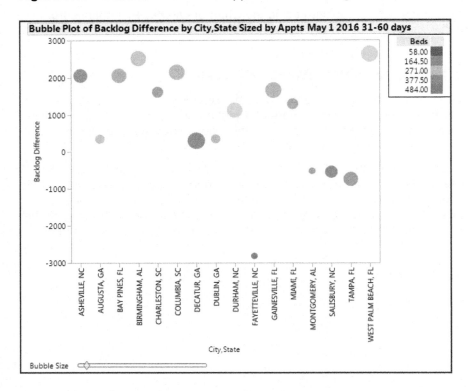

The plot can be enhanced by adding a reference line at 0 on the y-axis to clearly delineate those hospitals whose backlog has increased and those whose backlog has decreased. This can be done by right clicking over any of the numbers on the y-axis scale and selecting Axis Settings. Type 0 into the Value field in the Reference Lines portion of the dialog and click Add. Note that a preview of the reference line appears to the right. The bubble plot with the added reference line is shown in Figure 9.14 on page 139.

Figure 9.14 *Bubble Plot for VHA Appointment Backlogs with Reference Line*

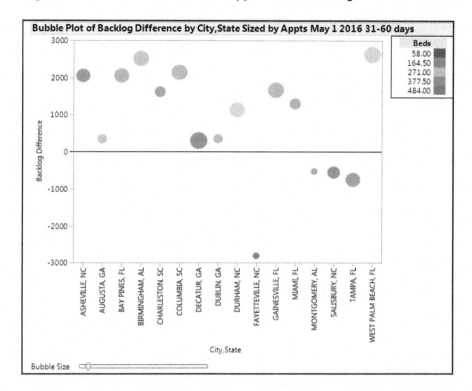

In this plot we see that the Fayetteville, NC facility has experienced a considerable reduction in backlog and that in 2016 it has a relatively small backlog of appointments over 31-60 days. Fayetteville has one of the smallest in-patient capacities. Six of the larger facilities appear to have had small changes in their backlogs relative to 2015. These facilities are generally, although not exclusively, larger sized facilities. Not surprisingly, large backlogs in 2016 are associated with increases in backlog over the previous year as shown by the larger circles at the top of the bubble plot.

Figure 9.15 on page 140 shows another view of the data by changing the size of the bubbles to indicate bed capacity and the color scale to indicate patient satisfaction ratings.

Figure 9.15 *Bubble Plot Showing Bed Capacity and Patient Satisfaction*

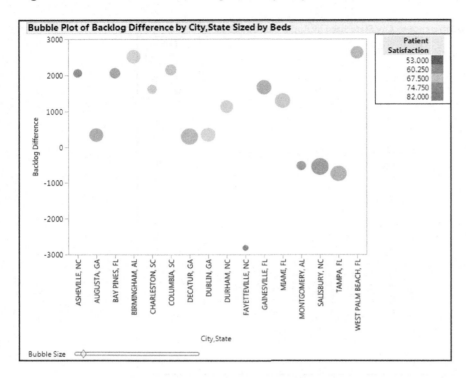

In this visualization we see that while the Fayetteville, NC facility appears to have improved their backlog performance over the year, it has one of the lowest patient satisfaction ratings. The two red-shaded bubbles are the hospitals with the highest patient satisfaction but had large increases in their backlog.

Multivariate Visualization: Geographic Maps

Presenting the 2016 backlog levels on a map allows the reader to interpret the data in geographic context. This can be done with the JMP Graph Builder. Drag Longitude to the X drop zone and Latitude to the Y drop zone. Select the Points button on the control panel. Right click over any one of the points and choose Graph > Background Map. Complete the Set Background Map dialog as shown in Figure 9.16 on page 141.

Figure 9.16 *Set Background Map Dialog*

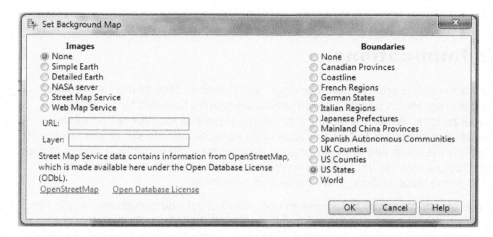

This will show US state borders on the map. Drag Beds to the Color drop zone and Appts May 1 2016 31-60 days to the Size drop zone. The dots over the location of each VA medical center will be sized to the magnitude of the backlog and the color scale will indicate the hospital's bed capacity. The map is shown in Figure 9.16 on page 141.

Figure 9.17 *Map of 2016 Appointment Backlog and Bed Capacities*

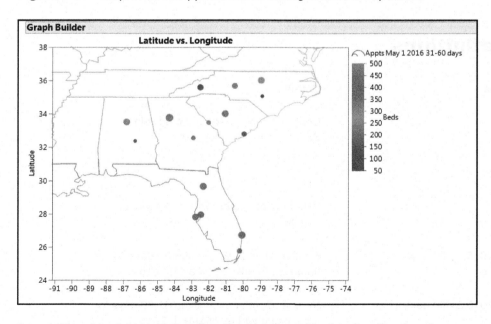

An additional variable can be visualized by dragging it to the Overlay drop zone. This additional variable will be rendered using symbols.

Analysis Implications

This initial exploration of the appointment backlogs and characteristics of the VA medical centers followed a progression beginning with univariate graphs followed by bivariate and multivariate visualizations. While it is tempting to jump right in and look for relationships between variables, it is important to first visualize each variable individually. Not only does it focus the analyst on the observed magnitude and variation for each variable, it allows outliers to be identified. Outliers may be unusual observations or data errors that warrant further investigation and in the case of data errors correction or removal.

Visualizations are an effective way to familiarize both the analyst and stakeholders with the data available for analysis and the variations between the VA hospitals. Plotting this information on a map adds geographic context. The exploratory analysis allows us to form initial impressions about the relationships between variables and develop hypotheses. However, it does not allow us to definitively answer questions such as "Has there been a significant change in the appointment backlogs from 2015 and 2016?" In the next case, we will make use of statistical tests of hypothesis to address such questions.

Data Definitions

Column Name	Definition
Provider ID	Centers for Medicare and Medicaid Services Provider Number
Hospital Name	
VISN	Veterans Integrated Service Network number
Appts May 1 2015 31-60 days	Number of veterans waiting 31-60 days for an appointment as of May 1, 2015
Appts May 1 2016 31-60 days	Number of veterans waiting 31-60 days for an appointment as of May 1, 2015
Address	Street address

Column Name	Definition
City	
State	US Postal Service abbreviation
Zip	US Postal Service zip code
County Name	
Latitude	
Longitude	
Phone Number	
Patient Satisfaction	Percentage of patients who gave the hospital a 9 or 10 rating on overall satisfaction from the Veterans Administration Inpatient Satisfaction Survey

Problems

1 Create bivariate graphs as shown in this case using the 2016 backlogs (Column Appts May 1 2016 31-60 days) as the y variable. Compare these charts to those shown in the case. How do the relationships differ? Experiment with other types of charts and graph options.

2 Create a bubble plot with State on the x-axis, Difference on the y-axis, Beds as the size, and color as Patient Satisfaction. Compare this plot to the map created in this case. Discuss the strengths and weaknesses of each of these plots.

3 Obtain the number of veterans waiting 31-60 days for an appointment for May 2, 2017. Add a new column to the data file VHA_appts.jmp for that data. Use Tables > Stack to create reformat the table so that there is a new column to indicate year. This format will enable you to animate a bubble plot over time. Create a bubble plot with four variables of your choice and animate it over the three years.

4 Choose another region of the country and randomly select 12-16 VA medical centers. Build a file similar to VHA_Appts.jmp. The information can be obtained from the Centers for Medicare and Medicaid Services and Department of Veterans Affairs websites. Recreate the plots presented in this case. How does this region compare to the southeast region?

10

Have Appointment Wait Times Changed at Veterans Medical Centers?

Chapter Summary Concepts

Statistical Concepts	Data Management Concepts	JMP Features
Descriptive Statistics	Derived Data	Column Information > Notes
Paired t-test	Data normalization into atomic elements	Tabulate
Outlier Analysis		Distribution
		Specialized Modeling > Matched Pairs
		Rows > Exclude
		Formula Editor

Background

Throughout their history, the various federal agencies charged with providing benefits and assistance to veterans have been plagued by a variety of scandals. Following World War II, several government commissions uncovered widespread waste and poor quality of care. The poor performance continued into the 1970s when veterans were frustrated by the Veterans Administration's reluctance to adequately fund treatment programs, particularly for the health consequences of exposure to the herbicide Agent Orange. In 1989 President Reagan created the Department of Veterans Affairs as a cabinet-level agency, but this still did not satisfactorily improve operations and patient care.

Since 2013 there have been continuing reports of long wait times for appointments at some Veterans Health Administration (VHA) medical centers and some deaths have been attributed to those delays. Other media and government investigations found that some VHA medical facilities were not in compliance with VHA scheduling policies and procedures and that scheduling information was being altered to show better performance than was actually occurring. In August 2014, President Obama signed a $16 billion bill to build more VHA facilities and to hire more health care providers. Disciplinary actions, including the firing of the Secretary of Veterans Affairs, were taken to address mismanagement within the VHA. Despite these efforts, the problem of long wait times for medical care at veterans' facilities continues.

In this case study we continue the analysis begun in the case "Appointment Wait Times at Veterans Medical Centers" to determine if there have been statistically significant changes in the appointment backlogs at VHA medical centers in the southeastern part of the United States.

Problem Statement

Has there been a significant change in the number of veterans waiting from 31-60 days for an appointment in the southeastern part of the United States from May 1, 2015 to May 1, 2016?

The Data

We will utilize the same data set as we did in the case "Appointment Wait Times at Veterans Medical Centers." The data was obtained from the Veterans Health Administration and the Centers for Medicare and Medicaid Services websites. The file VHA_Appts_Processed.jmp was created manually from these various data sources and contains the derived data added in the case "Appointment Wait Times at Veterans Medical Centers."

The 16 veterans medical centers (VMC) represented in the data are a sample from three of the Veterans Integrated Service Networks (Mid-Atlantic (VISN 6), Southeast (VISN 7), and Sunshine (VISN 8)) that serve veterans in the southeast United States. Pertinent information about the various columns is documented through JMP Notes (Right click on the column name and select Column Properties > Notes).

Data Management

No further data processing is required for the file VHA_Appts_Processed.jmp for this case. Notice that each element of the hospital's address is stored as a separate column. Storing the elements in separate columns is a best practice in data management. It is easier to create derived data elements by combining columns rather than parsing a single column that contains the entire address. In the previous case we created such derived data by combining the city and state columns. Different uses of the data (e.g., reports, analyzes) may require hospital address to be expressed in different formats. Having each address element separately also facilities analysis. For example, backlog difference can be easily analyzed by state or VISN.

Analytic Approach

In this case study we would like to determine if there has been a significant change in the number of veterans waiting from 31-60 days for an appointment in the southeastern part of the United States from May 1, 2015 to May 1, 2016?

The three questions below will guide the selection of appropriate methods.

1 What is the response (Y) of interest and how is it measured? We are interested in understanding the change in the appointment backlogs from May 1, 2015 to May 1, 2016. The column Backlog Difference contains this change. It is a continuous variable.

2 Are predictor variables mentioned in the problem statement? If so, how many and what are their measurement levels? The research question asks if there has been a change in the backlog over a year. The predictor is time, a nominal variable, measured at two points in time.

3 What are you being asked to deliver? A data description, an interval estimate, an answer to a question, or a predictive model? We are being asked to answer a question regarding the change in backlog over a year. A test of hypothesis will establish if the average change in backlog is statistically significant.

JMP Analysis

Descriptive Analysis

The case "Appointment Wait Times at Veterans Medical Centers" presented a variety of univariate, bivariate, and multivariate visualizations to become acquainted with the appointment backlogs and the characteristics of each medical center (e.g., bed capacity, location). While graphs allow us to easily discern patterns, numerical statistics offer a more precise measure of various characteristics of the distribution of each variable.

A number of the variables, such as Provider ID, Hospital Name, and the address columns, are unique identifiers associated with each veterans medical center, so a statistical summary of these columns is not warranted. The key variables are those relating to the appointment backlog.

Tables of numerical statistics can be easily generated from Tabulate. Drag the columns containing backlog data to the drop zone for rows. The Sum will appear as a default. Drag "Sum" to the empty column heading above the numbers. Now select N, Mean, Std Dev, Min, and Max and drag them to the column header occupied by Sum. The result is shown in Figure 10.1 on page 149.

Figure 10.1   *Tabulate for Backlog Variables*

Tabulate

	N	Mean	Std Dev	Min	Max
Appts May 1 2015 31-60 days	16	2182.4375	1243.4586693976	467	4644
Appts May 1 2016 31-60 days	16	3025.6875	1389.110301296	771	4946
Backlog Difference	16	843.25	1475.9733737	-2815	2625

The statistics should be rounded. Given the magnitude of the backlog values, we will round them all to the nearest integer. At the bottom of the Tabulate dialog click on the Change Format button and complete the dialog as shown in Figure 10.2 on page 149.

Figure 10.2   *Changing Tabulate Formats*

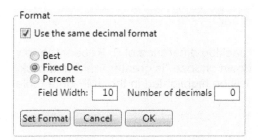

The table with rounded values is shown in Figure 10.3 on page 149.

Figure 10.3   *Table of Descriptive Statistics for Backlog Variables*

Tabulate

	N	Mean	Std Dev	Min	Max
Appts May 1 2015 31-60 days	16	2182	1243	467	4644
Appts May 1 2016 31-60 days	16	3026	1389	771	4946
Backlog Difference	16	843	1476	-2815	2625

Depending on the problem, other descriptive statistics may be informative. The minimum observed backlog difference is negative which means that at least one VMC reduced their 31-60 day backlog. Similarly, the positive maximum value indicates that at least one VMC's backlog increased from 2015 to 2016. Calculating the percentage of VMCs in the sample that are unchanged, decreased and increased their backlogs will add insight. To find any VMCs whose backlog has not changed, Choose Rows > Row Selection > Select Where and complete the dialog as shown in Figure 10.4 on page 150 to see if there are any VMCs that had no change in backlog.

Figure 10.4   *Selecting Rows with Backlog Difference of Zero*

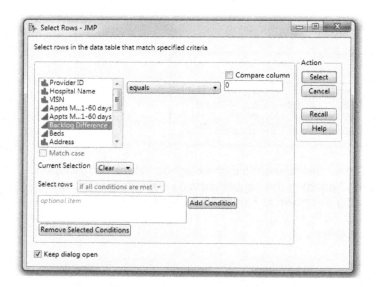

No rows are selected, so there are no hospital with a backlog difference of 0. Repeat the row selection process but this time from the criteria drop-down choose "is greater than" and click OK. Rows with Backlog Difference greater than zero will be highlighted in the JMP data table as shown in Figure 10.5 on page 151.

Figure 10.5 *JMP Data Table with Backlog Difference Greater than Zero Selected*

	Provider ID	Hospital Name	VISN	Appts May 1 2015 31-60 days	Appts May 1 2016 31-60 days	Backlog Difference	Beds	Address
1	34012F	DURHAM VA ME...	6	2947	4077	1130	271	508 FULTON STR...
2	34013F	FAYETTEVILLE NC...	6	3586	771	-2815	58	2300 RAMSEY ST...
3	34036F	ASHEVILLE-OTEE...	6	1251	3310	2059	119	1100 TUNNEL RO...
4	34017F	W.G. (BILL) HEFN...	6	3147	2599	-548	484	1601 BRENNER A...
5	11029F	DECATUR (ATLA...	7	4644	4946	302	466	1670 CLAIRMON...
6	11030F	AUGUSTA VA ME...	7	1196	1544	348	315	950 15TH STREET
7	01014F	BIRMINGHAM V...	7	1545	4061	2516	313	700 SOUTH 19TH...
8	42029F	CHARLESTON VA...	7	467	2085	1618	145	109 BEE STREET
9	42011F	COLUMBIA SC V...	7	2062	4212	2150	204	6439 GARNERS F...
10	11031F	DUBLIN VA MEDI...	7	1165	1519	354	340	1826 VETERANS ...
11	01019F	VA CENTRAL ALA...	7	1349	827	-522	143	215 PERRY HILL R...
12	10009F	BAY PINES VA M...	8	1695	3754	2059	186	10000 BAY PINES...
13	10064F	MIAMI VA MEDI...	8	832	2127	1295	372	1201 N W 16TH ...
14	10065F	W PALM BEACH ...	8	2089	4714	2625	270	7305 N. MILITAR...
15	10057F	VA NORTH FLORI...	8	2660	4325	1665	350	1601 S W ARCHE...
16	10063F	TAMPA VA MEDI...	8	4284	3540	-744	415	13000 BRUCE B D...

At the left of the data table we see that there are 12 rows selected out of 16. Twelve out of 16, or 75% of the VMCs saw increases in their backlogs over a year, while 25% reduced their backlogs. These percentages should be included in the statistical summary of the data. Using Rows > Row Selection > Select Where is often easier when there are precise numerical criteria. The slider bar available in the Rows > Data Filter may be more difficult for selecting the precise numerical value desired.

Another way to describe the backlog data is to look at the relative change from 2015 to 2016. This can be done by creating a new column, called Percent Backlog Change using the Formula Editor. Figure 10.6 on page 152 shows the completed Formula Editor where the percent change is rounded to one decimal place.

Figure 10.6   *Formula Editor to Create Percent Backlog Change Column*

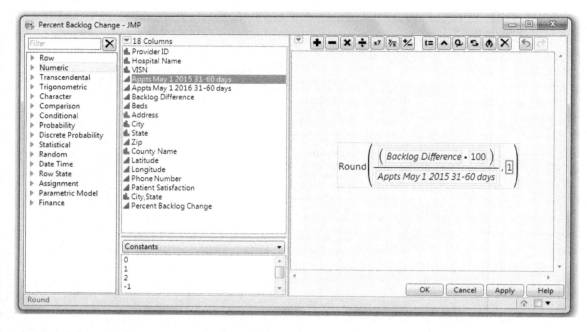

The Percent Backlog Change column is described using the Distribution platform as shown in Figure 10.7 on page 152.

Figure 10.7   *Data Description for Percent Backlog Change*

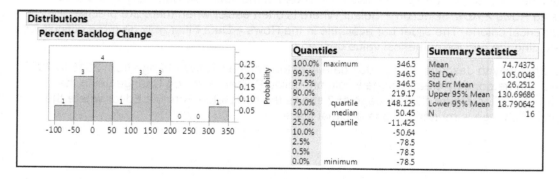

The percent backlog change shows that some VMCs more than doubled their backlog, while in the best case, one VMC decreased the backlog by close to 80%.

In this section we have showed a variety of ways to summarize the backlog data numerically. When presenting a statistical summary, select the view of the data that is consistent with the problem statement and will be most easily understood by your audience.

Selecting the Hypothesis Test

The problem statement can be addressed with a statistical test of hypothesis. We need to choose the statistical parameter that will be used to answer the research question. Since we are interested in the change in the level of the backlog, the mean is an appropriate statistic.

Two backlogs at two time periods are being compared so a t-test is the appropriate method. There are two forms of the t-test, paired comparisons and two independent samples. Which form of the t-test to apply depends on the nature of the test subjects (the hospitals) and how the data was collected. Paired comparisons are applicable when the test subjects are different in some way. For example, the hospitals are of different sizes. Paired comparisons are also applicable when the "treatment" can be repeated on the same subject. This method has the advantage of reducing variation due to individual differences in the test subjects. A two sample t-test is indicated when the treatment destroys the test specimen, when there is no natural pairing, or for a variety of other reasons.

Experience suggests that there are differences between hospitals in terms of their bed capacity, facility age, the number and type of services offered, staffing levels, and management. Figure 10.8 on page 153 gives a statistical summary of the bed capacity of the hospitals in the sample obtained from the JMP Distribution platform.

Figure 10.8 *Descriptive Analysis of Bed Capacity*

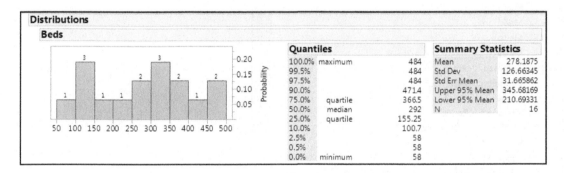

The Summary Statistics table can be customized by selecting Customize Summary Statistics from the drop-down menu next to the Summary Statistics heading. The menu of options appears as shown in Figure 10.9 on page 154 where the mean, standard deviation, sample size (N), and median have been chosen.

Figure 10.9 *Summary Statistics Options*

Figure 10.10 on page 155 shows the customized table of summary statistics where we see that the bed capacity spans almost an order of magnitude for this sample.

Figure 10.10 *Customized Summary Statistics for VMC Bed Capacities*

Distributions

Beds

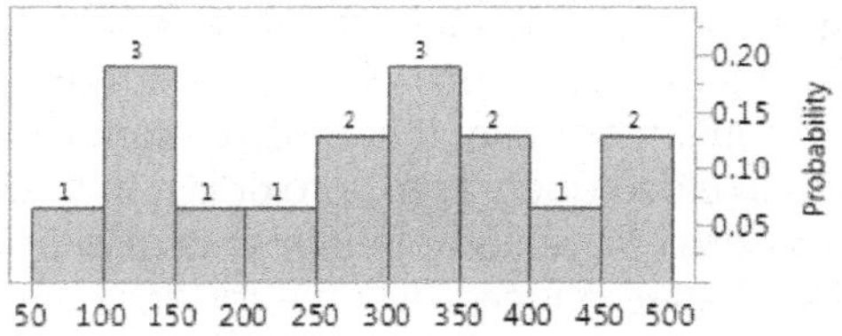

Quantiles

100.0%	maximum	484
99.5%		484
97.5%		484
90.0%		471.4
75.0%	quartile	366.5
50.0%	median	292
25.0%	quartile	155.25
10.0%		100.7
2.5%		58
0.5%		58
0.0%	minimum	58

Summary Statistics

Mean	278.1875
Std Dev	126.66345
N	16
Minimum	58
Maximum	484
Median	292

Default summary statistics can be set from File > Preferences > Platforms > Distribution Summary Statistics.

The analysis of bed capacity confirms our intuition that the VMCs are heterogeneous. We also see in Figure 10.3 on page 149 that the 2015 backlogs, the baseline for comparison, vary almost an order of magnitude. There is a natural pairing between the backlogs for 2015 and 2016 and the hospitals are heterogeneous, so a paired comparison is the appropriate t-test to apply.

Setting Up the Hypotheses

In a paired comparison, the difference between the 2015 and 2016 backlogs will be analyzed. The subtraction removes the variation due to the inherent differences in the hospitals. The column Backlog Difference was created in the case "Appointment Wait Times at Veterans Medical Centers" and it is the mean of this variable that we will analyze.

The null hypothesis assumes that there is no change on average in the backlog level, i.e., the mean backlog difference is equal to zero. The alternative hypothesis could be two-sided which would detect a change in the backlog mean in either a negative or positive direction. There are two possibilities for a one-sided alternative, either looking for only an increase or only a decrease in the mean backlog.

Since the VA is under pressure to improve their performance, it would seem that a one-sided alternative to detect a reduction in the mean backlog should be chosen. However, if there has in fact been a significant increase in the mean backlog, this form of the alternative hypothesis will not detect that. A two-sided alternative will detect if there has been a significant change, either an increase or a decrease in the mean backlog. A two-sided alternative is consistent with the phrasing of the problem statement. The choice of the alternative hypothesis should reflect the problem statement.

Checking Paired t-test Assumptions

Prior to performing a hypothesis test it is good practice to check the associated assumptions. Violation of the assumptions can result in drawing incorrect conclusions which can lead to unwarranted problem domain recommendations or actions. The paired t-test assumptions are independent samples and that the differences are normally distributed.

In a paired comparison, it is expected that the two observations are dependent. In this case, the size of the backlog at a hospital in 2016 will depend on what the backlog was in 2015. The independence assumption is for the relationship between the test subjects, or in this case the hospitals. The degree to which this assumption is satisfied will not come from a statistical test, but rather an understanding of the problem domain. It seems reasonable that the backlogs could be related for hospitals that are in close geographic proximity. In these situations, patients in that geographic region could easily travel to appointments at either hospital and may choose between the two hospitals based on the wait time for an appointment. In the case, "Appointment Wait Times at Veterans Medical Centers" a map was created showing the locations, bed capacity, and 2015 appointment backlog. This map is reproduced in Figure 10.11 on page 156.

Figure 10.11 Map Showing VMC Locations, Bed Capacity, and 2015 Appointment Backlog

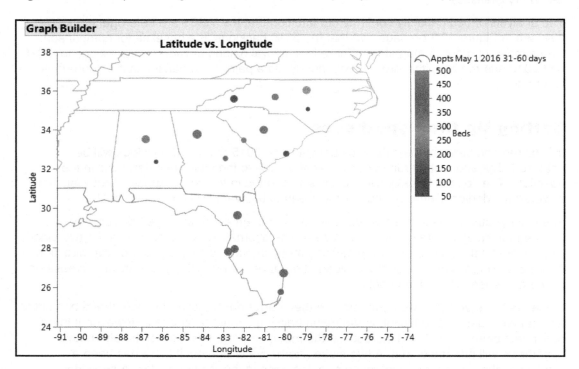

The map shows that only two hospitals on the West coast of Florida are within close proximity where dependence may exist between their backlogs. Further investigation into other aspects of these two hospitals such as similarity of services offered can help establish if their backlogs can be reasonably considered independent. Such information can be readily obtained from the websites for these two VMCs.

The normality assumption for the Backlog Difference can be assessed from the JMP Distribution platform in two different ways. Figure 10.12 on page 157 shows a normal quantile plot for Backlog Difference obtained from the Backlog Difference drop-down menu.

Figure 10.12 *Normal Quantile Plot of Backlog Difference*

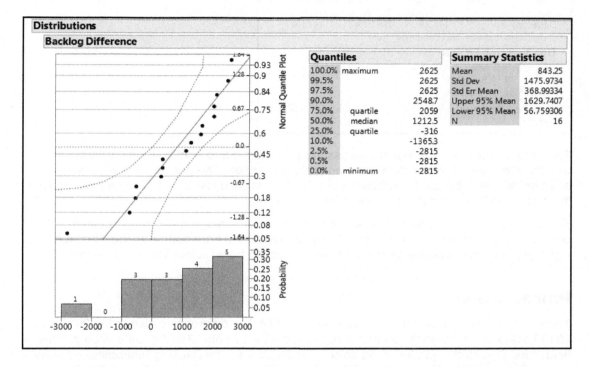

In the Normal quantile plot, the line corresponds to the Normal distribution that best fits the data. The Normality assumption is satisfied to the extent that the observations lie close to this line. The observed backlog differences fall reasonably close to this line with the exception of the minimum observed backlog of -2815 which corresponds to the Fayetteville, NC VMC.

The JMP Distribution platform also provides the Shapiro-Wilk Normality test as an option to assess normality. From the Backlog Difference drop-down select Continuous Fit > Normal and the Fitted Normal output will appear. From the Fitted Normal drop-down select Goodness of Fit. Figure 10.13 on page 158 shows the corresponding output.

Figure 10.13 *Shapiro-Wilk Normality Test Output for Backlog Difference*

Fitted Normal

Parameter Estimates

Type	Parameter	Estimate	Lower 95%	Upper 95%
Location	μ	843.25	56.759306	1629.7407
Dispersion	σ	1475.9734	1090.3087	2284.351

-2log(Likelihood) = 277.912367959464

Goodness-of-Fit Test

Shapiro-Wilk W Test

W	Prob<W
0.915178	0.1410

Note: Ho = The data is from the Normal distribution. Small p-values reject Ho.

The Shapiro-Wilk test null hypothesis assumes the data come from a Normal distribution, with the alternative that the data is not normally distributed. The p-value of 0.1410 is not sufficient to reject the null hypothesis at the 5% significance level. Therefore, we can assume the backlog difference data is normally distributed.

The assumptions for the paired t-test are reasonably satisified and we can proceed to conduct the paired t-test. In the case of a severe departure from normality, the Wilcoxon signed-rank test is available as a nonparametric option from Distribution > Test Mean.

Paired t-test

There are two ways to perform a paired t-test in JMP. The difference between the 2015 and 2016 backlogs can be analyzed with a one-sample t-test. Enter Backlog Difference into the Y field in the Distribution platform and select Test Mean from the Backlog Difference drop-down menu. Enter 0 for the Hypothesized Mean. The JMP output is shown in Figure 10.14 on page 158.

Figure 10.14 *JMP Test Mean Output for Backlog Difference*

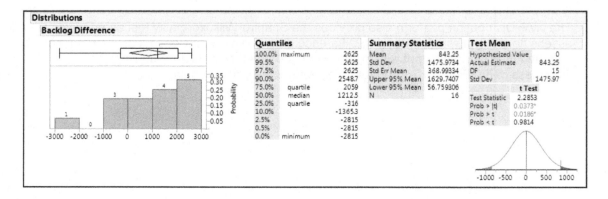

On average, the backlog has increased by 843 for the Southeast United States. The t-test will tell us if this change is statistically significant. The key result from a hypothesis test is the p-value. JMP gives three p-values, one associated with each of the three possible alternative hypotheses. In this case, we are using a two-sided alternative so Prob > |t| = 0.0373 is the corresponding p-value. The p-value is the likelihood of obtaining the sample mean or something more extreme assuming the null hypothesis is true. Small p-values cause a rejection of the null hypothesis. In this case, the null hypothesis can be rejected at the 5% level and we can conclude that there has been a change in mean backlog from 2015 to 2016. In fact the backlog has increased, not the desired outcome from the perspective of the Veterans' Administration and veterans seeking improvements in appointment waiting times.

The second way to conduct a paired t-test is from Analyze > Specialized Modeling > Matched Pairs. It gives the same numerical results as Distribution > Test Mean and has the advantage of providing additional graphical output and does not require a column (and formula) to hold the difference. The completed dialog to perform a paired t-test from JMP's Matched Pairs is shown in Figure 10.15 on page 159.

Figure 10.15   *Completed Matched Pairs Dialog*

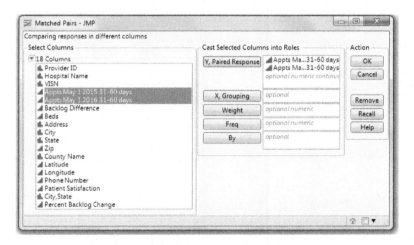

From the Matched Pairs drop-down select Plot Dif by Row. Figure 10.16 on page 160 shows the Matched Pairs output.

Figure 10.16 Matched Pairs Output

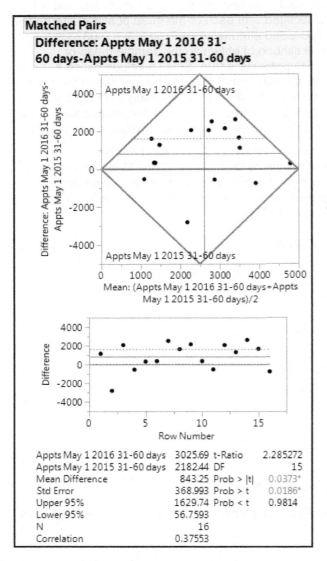

The differences plotted by row show clearly the large reduction in the backlog for the Fayetteville, NC VMC. For small sample sizes, outliers can have substantial influence on the results. To assess the influence this outlier, exclude the Fayetteville, NC observation by highlighting the corresponding row in the JMP data table, right click and select Exclude. This will exclude the Fayetteville backlog from the paired t-test but it will remain in the graphs. The Hide option will prevent a highlighted row from being displayed in JMP graphs. The estimated mean difference is now 1087. Excluding the Fayetteville observation does not change the hypothesis test conclusion (p-value = 0.0025).

Analysis Implications

In this case we made use of a paired t-test to establish that there was a statistically significant change in the mean number of veterans waiting 31-60 days for an appointment from a sample of Southeastern US veterans medical centers. A paired comparison was the appropriate analysis since there is a natural pairing between each hospital's 2015 and 2016 backlogs and the VMCs are not homogeneous.

Stakeholders are hoping for improvement in the performance of VMCs with respect to delays in treating veterans in need of care. However, it is important to formulate the problem statement and hypothesis test in a way that will detect a change in performance, either improvement or degradation, over the course of a year. While measures were taken to reduce the backlogs, they may not have been effective. Other possible reasons for the increased backlog could be increased demand for service or decreased staffing levels (a problem that has also be reported in the VA medical system).

The test of hypothesis established the statistically significant increase, but examining the graphs showed that Fayetteville, NC was the only VMC that achieved a substnatial reduction in backlog. Outliers can influence the outcome of a hypothesis test. A statistically significant difference can be obtained with the outlier included in the analysis, but excluding the outlier results in a difference that is not significantly different and vice versa. In small sample sizes, outliers can be particularly influential. From a statistical viewpoint, outliers should be investigated to look for possible causes such as a data collection error. From the perspective of the problem domain, investigating an outlier that is not found to be in error may provide valuable insights. For example, Fayetteville may be doing something differently than the other VMCs that is effective in reducing the backlogs.

In this case we analyzed only one facet of the problem, the change in the 31-60 backlog. The VA provides information on the number of veterans waiting both shorter and longer periods of time for appointments. While there appears to be an increase across the Southwest US, the data set contains additional variables that can be analyzed. For example, are there differences between VISNs or states? How does bed capacity affect the backlog? More detailed analysis should be conducted so that a complete understanding of the problem is obtained. To improve performance it is important to understand if problems are systematic or related to another factor such as VISN, state, or bed capacity. This will enable targeted improvement actions to be developed.

Data Definitions

Column Name	Definition
Provider ID	Centers for Medicare and Medicaid Services Provider Number
Hospital Name	
VISN	Veterans Integrated Service Network number
Appts May 1 2015 31-60 days	Number of veterans waiting 31-60 days for an appointment as of May 1, 2015
Appts May 1 2016 31-60 days	Number of veterans waiting 31-60 days for an appointment as of May 1, 2015
Backlog Difference	The change in the number of veterans waiting 31-60 days for an appointment from May 1, 2015 to May 1, 2016.
Address	Street address
City	
State	US Postal Service abbreviation
Zip	US Postal Service zip code
County Name	
Latitude	
Longitude	
Phone Number	

Column Name	Definition
Patient Satisfaction	Percentage of patients who gave the hospital a 9 or 10 rating on overall satisfaction from the Veterans Administration Inpatient Satisfaction Survey
City.State	The city and state where the veterans' medical center is located.

Problems

1 Prepare a one-page summary of the VA appointments data including the backlog and hospital characteristics. Include a combination of graphs and numerical statistics that you think effectively summarizes the data. Discuss the rationale for your choices.

2 Choose another region of the country and randomly select 12-16 VA medical centers from three or four VISNs. Build a file similar to VA_Appts_Processed.jmp. Repeat the analysis from this case. How do the results for this region compare to those of the southeast region?

3 Given the results of the analyses conducted in this case, what would you recommend as a next analysis using the given data? Is there other data that you think would be helpful to better understand the change in backlog?

11

Health Care Costs for Newborns in Adirondack Hospitals

Chapter Summary Concepts

Statistical Concepts	Data Management Concepts	JMP Features
Outlier analysis	Data formatting	Import non-JMP files
Data visualization • Histogram • Scatterplot • Dot plot • Log scaling	Data dictionary	Column Viewer
Descriptive statistics		List Check
Cross-tabulation		JMP Project
		Recode
		Graph Builder

Background

The Northeast region of New York is dominated by the Adirondack Park, created by the State of New York in 1892 for the purpose of conserving water and timber resources. The park encompasses approximately 6 million acres, half of which are owned by New York State and protected as "forever wild." The other half of the park is privately owned. The Adirondack Park Agency closely regulates land use and development to preserve the natural beauty and resources. The region is sparsely populated and the economy is driven by tourism. Today the region faces a number of challenges including poverty, an aging population, limited broadband access, and a shortage of clinicians.

Problem Statement

In this case we will explore data associated with newborns at hospitals in the Adirondack region in 2014 with a primary interest in identifying factors related to total costs for inpatient stays.

The Data

SPARCS (Statewide Planning and Research Cooperative System) data is patient-level health care data collected by New York State for the purpose of providing health care organizations with information that will enable them to efficiently and cost effectively deliver services. This data reporting system was established in 1979 and collects data on patient characteristics, diagnoses, treatments, and services for inpatient, ambulatory surgery, emergency department admission, and outpatient visits. The full data set contains personally identifiable information and as such access is carefully controlled. A subset of the inpatient discharge data is made available to the public. We will use this de-identified data for 2014 to examine the total cost associated with newborns. SPARCS provides a web interface that allows subsets of the data to be downloaded in a variety of formats. The file ADK_Newborns_2014.xlsx was downloaded directly from SPARCS and contains the information on newborns born in hospitals in the Adirondack region. A data dictionary was also downloaded from SPARCS that gives the definition of each variable. Total costs are the actual cost of the services provided; total charges are the amounts charged to insurers.

Data Management

Importing an Excel File into JMP

JMP can import files from a variety of formats. From the JMP menu select File > Open. In the Open Data File dialog navigate to the desired folder where ADK_Newborns_2014.xslx is stored and select "Excel files" from the file type drop-down menu. This will display the available Excel files. Select ADK_Newborns_2014.xslx then click OK and the Excel Import Wizard will appear as shown in Figure 11.1 on page 168.

Figure 11.1 Excel Import Wizard

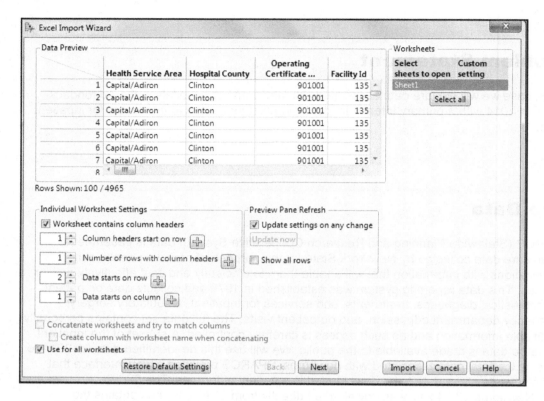

The wizard shows a preview of how the Excel data will appear in a JMP data table. Adjustments can be made in the wizard to indicate the number of rows in the Excel file that contain headers and the row and column where the data begins. Click the Import button to open the JMP data table.

Checking and Reformatting the Imported JMP Columns

Once the data is imported into JMP, the columns should be checked to be sure that they have the correct data and modeling types. There is no guarantee that the data elements as stored in the native file format are as needed for the JMP analysis. Other column formatting such as List Check may need to be applied.

The Data Table Columns Viewer is a convenient way to quickly review the modeling types that were assigned to each column on import. Select Cols > Column Viewer and a list of columns appears. The column Operating Certification Number is an identifier and should be changed to a nominal modeling type. This can be done by right clicking over the modeling type icon and choosing "Nominal" as shown in Figure 11.2 on page 169.

Figure 11.2 *Changing the Modeling Type in Data Table Columns Viewer*

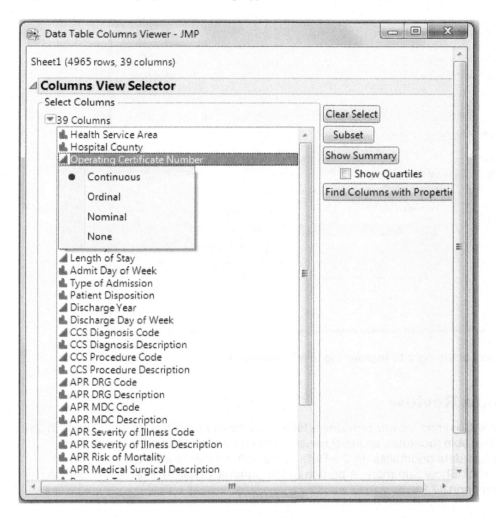

Some of the columns, such as APR Risk of Mortality, contain ordinal variables. The levels or ordinal variables can be ordered using the List Check column property. This is done for APR Risk of Mortality by right clicking in the column header and choosing Column Info and from that dialog select List Check from the Column Properties drop-down menu. Figure 11.3 on page 170 shows the List Check dialog.

Figure 11.3 *List Check Dialog for APR Risk of Mortality Column*

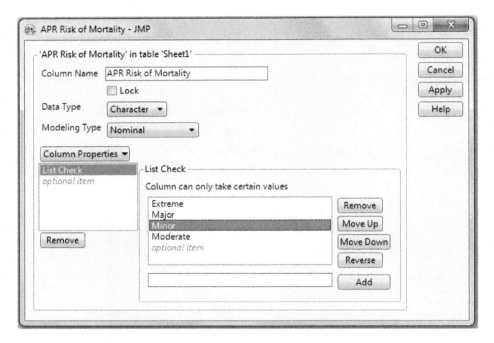

Use the buttons at the right to reorder the levels as desired.

Initial Data Review

The Data Table Columns Viewer provides a table of summary statistics for all columns in the data table. This table facilitates an initial review of the data to ascertain the amount of missing data and data anomalies. In the Data Table Columns Viewer select all of the columns and click Show Summary. A portion of the Summary Statistics table is shown in Figure 11.4 on page 171.

Figure 11.4 *Columns Viewer Summary Statistics Table*

Columns	N	N Missing	N Categories	Min	Max	Mean	Std Dev
Health Service Area	4965	0	1				
Hospital County	4965	0	7				
Operating Certificate Number	4965	0		901001	5601000	3451765.45639476	1731940.40045245
Facility Id	4965	0		135	1005	629.535347432024	318.145345918237
Facility Name	4965	0	8				
Age Group	4965	0	1				
Zip Code - 3 digits	4965	0	20				
Gender	4965	0	3				
Race	4965	0	3				
Ethnicity	4965	0	3				
Length of Stay	4965	0		1	28	2.24531722054381	1.29363435792729
Admit Day of Week	4965	0	7				
Type of Admission	4965	0	4				
Patient Disposition	4965	0	7				
Discharge Year	4965	0		2014	2014	2014	0
Discharge Day of Week	4965	0	7				
CCS Diagnosis Code	4965	0		218	218	218	0
CCS Diagnosis Description	4965	0	1				
CCS Procedure Code	4965	0		0	231	118.523867069486	91.2683529629487
CCS Procedure Description	4965	0	22				

The sample size and number of missing values are given for each variable. The number of categories are displayed for nominal and ordinal columns. Descriptive statistics are displayed for continuous variables which allows identification of outliers.

Several columns such as Health Service Area have only one category. Selecting that column and clicking the Distribution button will display the JMP Distribution platform which shows all rows in this column have the value "Capital/Adiron". This column will not be useful in the analysis as it has no variation and if desired can be deleted to reduce the size of the data table.

There are pairs of related variables such as CCS Diagnosis Code and CCS Diagnosis Description. Codes facilitate data input but are not useful to analysts or stakeholders unfamiliar with the meaning of the code numbers. A separate column gives the description of the code. This architecture is a best practice in data management. If a coded column is not useful in the analysis or presentation of results, it can be deleted from the JMP data table.

Creating a JMP Project

A JMP project is a convenient way to maintain all documents related to an analysis. This is consistent with best practices of reproducible analysis and is efficient for the analyst or researcher who wishes to revisit this work in the future. A number of objects can be included in a JMP project including documents, URLs, JMP windows, and database queries.

To create a JMP project select File > New > Project and click on the New Project icon. A project is added with the name "Untitled." Right click the drop-down menu as shown in Figure 11.5 on page 172 to view the list of actions that can be taken.

Figure 11.5 JMP Project Menu

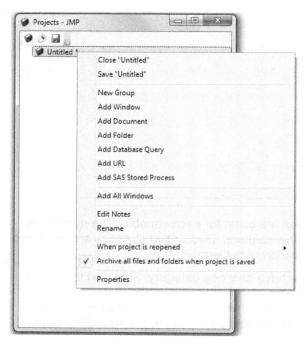

Figure 11.6 on page 172 shows the contents of the project named "ADK_Newborns_2014" which includes the URL to access the SPARCS 2014 data dictionary, the Excel file downloaded from SPARCS, the processed JMP file, and a JMP Distribution analysis of Birthweight. The URL was lengthy, so the entry was renamed by right clicking over the URL and selecting Rename from the menu.

Figure 11.6 Populated JMP Project

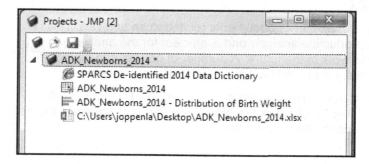

The file ADK_Newborns_2014.jmp contains a subset of the downloaded Excel data that will be used in this and subsequent cases. Several of the facility names have been shortened using the JMP Recode feature. This will improve the readability of graphs that use Facility Name. The data is now prepared and supporting documents are organized so the exploratory analysis can begin. Several of the JMP column names have been edited to include units.

Analytic Approach

The three questions below will guide the selection of appropriate methods to explore the data for newborns' hospital stays in the Adirondack region in 2014 with a primary objective of identifying factors related to total cost.

1 What is the response (Y) of interest and how is it measured? The variable of primary interest is total cost which is a continuous variable.

2 Are predictor variables mentioned in the problem statement? If so, how many and what are their measurement levels? The problem statement asks for the information on newborns to be explored with a focus on total costs. There are a number of nominal, ordinal, and continuous variables in the data set that may be related to total cost.

3 What are you being asked to deliver? A data description, an interval estimate, an answer to a question, or a predictive model? You are being asked to explore the newborn data as related to total cost for an inpatient hospital stay. Visualization is an effective way to identify and display possible relationships that are candidates for more detailed analysis.

JMP Analysis

Univariate Descriptive Analysis

At the beginning of an exploratory analysis, visualizing each variable individually will familiarize the analyst with the variation in each variable, assist in identifying outliers that should be investigated, and suggest variables that are related to total costs, the primary focus of our analysis. Figure 11.7 on page 174 shows the histograms for total costs, length of stay, and birthweight (in grams).

Figure 11.7 *Histograms for Total Costs, Length of Stay, Birthweight*

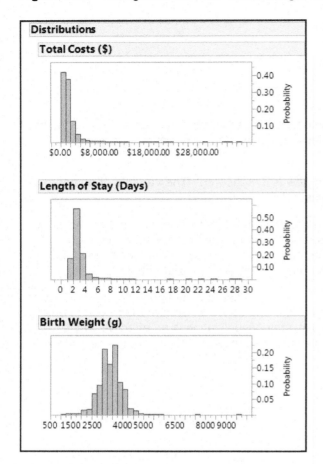

The distributions of total costs and length of stay are both right-skewed. Experience suggests that longer lengths of stay and higher costs are due to complications. Severe complications requiring lengthy hospital stays are relatively infrequent for these Adirondack hospitals. The birthweight is roughly bell-shaped with several very high values. Figure 11.8 on page 174 gives a table of descriptive statistics for these three variables.

Figure 11.8 *Descriptive Statistics for Total Costs, Length of Stay, Birthweight*

Tabulate						
	N	Mean	Median	Std Dev	Min	Max
Total Costs ($)	4965	$1,609	$1,159	1727	$252	$36,037
Length of Stay (Days)	4965	2.2	2.0	1.3	1.0	28.0
Birth Weight (g)	4965	3365	3400	512	1200	9600

The maximum birthweight of 9600 grams (21.2 lbs.) does not seem to be a reasonable weight for a newborn. Returning to the JMP data table and examining the corresponding record shows that this newborn was a female born at Saratoga Hospital with a one day length of stay, an extreme severity of illness and a moderate mortality risk. The total cost for the one day stay was $995.67. When dispositioning outliers, consulting external references can be of assistance. The CDC Clinical Growth Charts give selected percentiles for the distribution of children's weights in the US population. The chart shows that the 97th percentile (the largest percentile available) for newborn females is approximately 9.5 lbs. Based on this information, it is possible that there is an error in this particular record since the weight is more than twice the 97th percentile from the CDC Clinical Growth Charts. Further consultation with the data provider can assist the analyst with determining how to reconcile this outlier.

Figure 11.9 on page 175 shows the distributions of Emergency Department Indicator and CCS Procedure Description. Notice that only one newborn was admitted through an emergency department, so this variable will not be useful in understanding total costs as it has virtually no variability.

Figure 11.9 *Frequency Distributions for Emergency Department Indicator and CCS Procedure Description*

Distributions

Emergency Department Indicator

Frequencies

Level	Count	Prob
N	4964	0.9998
Y	1	0.0002
Total	4965	1.0000

N Missing 0

2 Levels

CCS Procedure Description

Frequencies

Level	Count	Prob
BLOOD TRANSFUSION	1	0.0002
CIRCUMCISION	1724	0.3472
CONV OF CARDIAC RHYTHM	3	0.0006
DIAGNOSTIC SPINAL TAP	6	0.0012
DX ULTRASOUND AB/RETRO	3	0.0006
DX ULTRASOUND HEAD/NECK	1	0.0002
DX ULTRASOUND URINARY	2	0.0004
NASOGASTRIC TUBE	1	0.0002
NO PROC	1467	0.2955
OPHTHALM-/OT-OLOGIC DX	57	0.0115
OT NON-OR THER PRC NOSE	51	0.0103
OT NON-OR THER PRC SKIN	5	0.0010
OT NON-OR UP GI THER PR	1	0.0002
OT THER PRCS ON MUSCLES	1	0.0002
OT VASC CATH; NOT HEART	6	0.0012
OTHER DX ULTRASOUND	8	0.0016
OTHER RESP THERAPY	8	0.0016
OTHER THERAPEUTIC PRCS	177	0.0356
PROPHYLACTIC VAC/INOCUL	1397	0.2814
RADIOISOTOPE BONE SCAN	1	0.0002
RESP INTUB/MECH VENTIL	43	0.0087
TRACHE-/LARYNG-OSCOPY	2	0.0004
Total	4965	1.0000

N Missing 0

22 Levels

Examining the CCS Procedure Description we see a large of number of procedures with a very few number of occurrences (e.g., nasogastric tube) and relatively high frequencies for circumcision, no procedure, and prophylactic vaccination. The low frequency procedures will be aggregated into a single level called "Other Procedures" using Cols > Recode. Highlight all of the low frequency procedures, and click the Group button, rename the group to "Other Procedures," and save as a new column. The new column "CCS Procedures Aggregated" has levels for circumcision, no procedure, prophylactic vaccination, and other procedures. Figure 11.10 on page 176 shows the distribution of this new column.

Figure 11.10   *Frequency Distributions for CCS Procedure Aggregated*

Distributions		
CCS Procedures Aggregated		
Frequencies		
Level	Count	Prob
CIRCUMCISION	1724	0.3472
NO PROC	1467	0.2955
OTHER PROCEDURES	377	0.0759
PROPHYLACTIC VAC/INOCUL	1397	0.2814
Total	4965	1.0000
N Missing	0	
4 Levels		

This new column will facilitate analysis of a potential relationship between total charges and no procedure, common procedures (circumcision and vaccination), and less commonly performed procedures.

Developing familiarity with the data one variable at a time helps guide the analyst when choosing variables for exploring bivariate and multivariate relationships.

Exploring Relationships with Total Costs: Length of Stay

In data sets with even a modest number of variables, there are many possible combinations that could be examined. A good strategy is to begin by examining bivariate relationships based on the problem statement, domain knowledge, and the univariate analysis. For example, the Emergency Department Indicator can be eliminated from consideration as described above. Graph Builder is a very flexible platform for visualizing relationships between variables. It offers a variety of different graphs and features for evaluating multivariate relationships.

Experience suggests that total costs are directly related to length of stay, so we will begin by visualizing this relationship. In Graph Builder, drag Length of Stay to the x drop zone and Total Costs to the y drop zone. The resulting scatterplot is shown in Figure 11.11 on page 177.

Figure 11.11 *Scatterplot of Length of Stay and Total Costs*

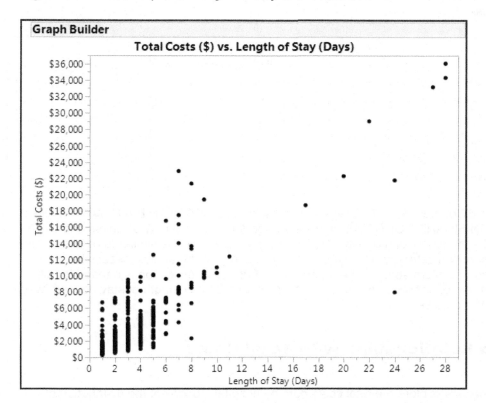

The relationship appears to follow a linear trend but there are a number of observations that are not consistent with this pattern. To identify particular observations, hover over a marker on the scatterplot. Selecting the marker will highlight the corresponding row in the data table. The observation for the 24 day length of stay with an approximate cost of $8000 corresponds to a male born at the Mary Imogene Bassett Hospital weighing 3900 grams (8 pounds 9.5 ounces) who had no procedure and an APR DRG Description of NEONATE BIRTHWT >2499G W OTHER SIGNIFICANT CONDITION, a minor APR severity of illness, and a minor APR risk of mortality. The All Patient Refined Diagnosis Related Groups is a classification system that links conditions to the resources consumed. This classification system has two subclassifications, severity of illness and risk of mortality, that are determined based on patient characteristics such as age and comorbidities. These classifications are used when determining payment.

To see how this newborn's severity of illness and mortality risk compare to other newborns with the same APR DRG description, a cross-tabulation (crosstab) can be created with the JMP Tabulate feature. Drag APR DRG Description into the drop zone for rows and APR Severity of Illness Description and APR Risk of Mortality to the drop zone for columns. Figure 11.12 on page 178 shows the crosstab.

Figure 11.12 Crosstab for Three Variables Classifying Diagnosis, Illness Severity, and Mortality Risk

Tabulate								
	APR Severity of Illness Description				APR Risk of Mortality			
APR DRG Description	Minor	Moderate	Major	Extreme	Minor	Moderate	Major	Extreme
NEONATE BIRTHWT >2499G W CONGENITAL/PERINATAL INFECTION	10	6	1	0	16	1	0	0
NEONATE BIRTHWT >2499G W MAJOR ANOMALY	50	5	0	0	51	3	1	0
NEONATE BIRTHWT >2499G W OTHER SIGNIFICANT CONDITION	67	3	0	0	70	0	0	0
NEONATE BIRTHWT >2499G, NORMAL NEWBORN OR NEONATE W OTHER PROBLEM	3970	502	97	0	4569	0	0	0
NEONATE BWT <500G	0	0	0	1	0	0	0	1
NEONATE BWT 1500-1999G W OR W/O OTHER SIGNIFICANT CONDITION	10	0	0	0	10	0	0	0
NEONATE BWT 2000-2499G W MAJOR ANOMALY	1	0	0	0	1	0	0	0
NEONATE BWT 2000-2499G W OTHER SIGNIFICANT CONDITION	4	0	0	0	4	0	0	0
NEONATE BWT 2000-2499G W RESP DIST SYND/OTH MAJ RESP COND	1	0	0	0	1	0	0	0
NEONATE BWT 2000-2499G, NORMAL NEWBORN OR NEONATE W OTHER PROBLEM	68	30	20	0	118	0	0	0
NEONATE, BIRTHWT >2499G W RESP DIST SYND/OTH MAJ RESP COND	15	2	0	0	17	0	0	0
NEONATE, TRANSFERRED < 5 DAYS OLD, BORN HERE	45	47	7	3	89	12	0	1

In this data set, 67 of the 70 (95.7%) newborns classified as NEONATE BIRTHWT >2499G W OTHER SIGNIFICANT CONDITION were assigned Minor for severity of illness and all 70 were assigned a minor risk of mortality. So the outlying observation is similar to others in this APR DRG Description category. This type of analysis can help the analyst assess the reasonableness of outliers absent other information. Further investigation is needed to fully understand the reason for the relatively low total cost for a 24 day length of stay beyond what is available in this data set.

Exploring Relationships with Total Costs: Hospital

In this section we will explore the total costs data by hospital. To look at the distribution of total costs by each of the eight hospitals select Graph Builder and drag Total Costs into the x drop zone and Facility Name into the y drop zone. Right click over any of the makers and select Add > Line. This line will connect a summary statistic (such as the mean or median) for each hospital distribution. Dropdown menus on the left allow customization of the line. "Jittering" the points will spread them out to better visualize the data density. This is particularly useful for large data sets. Since the cost distributions are right skewed, we will choose the median as the summary statistic. The mean is sensitive to the large outliers, while the median is not. Figure 11.13 on page 179 shows the completed Graph Builder dialog.

Figure 11.13 *Dot Plot of Total Costs by Hospital*

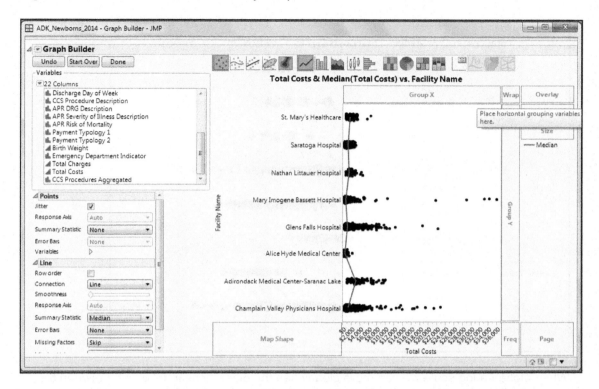

In this display, the costs for the hospitals are displayed on the same x-axis scale and we see that the costs span several orders of magnitude. Some of the distributions are highly right skewed which determines the x-axis range and makes visual comparison between the hospitals difficult. Viewing the cost data on a log scale will make visual comparison easier as it will spread out the left side of the cost distributions. To change the x-axis to a log scale right click on the x-axis and select Axis Setting. In the X Axis Settings dialog change the Scale Type to Log and set the Minimum to 100. The graph with a log scale is displayed in Figure 11.14 on page 180.

Figure 11.14 *Dot Plot of Total Costs by Hospital on a Log Scale*

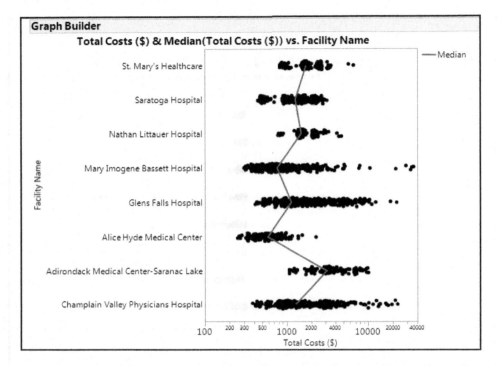

When plotted a log scale we can more clearly see the differences in total cost between the hospitals. The Champlain Valley Physicians, Mary Imogene Bassett, and Glens Falls hospitals display the most variation in total costs. The Adirondack Medical Center – Saranac Lake has the highest median cost while the Alice Hyde Hospital has the lowest.

The graph in Figure 11.14 on page 180 can be enhanced by dragging Length of Stay to the x axis drop zone to create side-by-side plots of Total Costs and Length of Stay by hospital. Plotted on a linear scale, Length of Stay distributions are right skewed for some hospitals, so the x-axis was changed to a log scale. The plot is shown in Figure 11.15 on page 181.

Figure 11.15 *Side-by-side Plots of Total Costs and Length of Stay by Hospital*

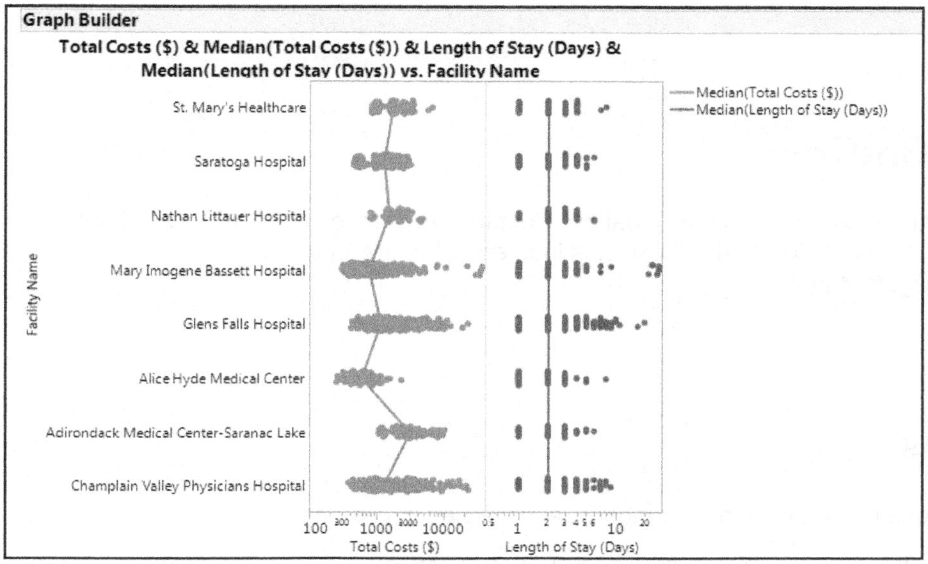

The length of stay is much less variable across the hospitals compared to total costs; all eight hospitals had a median length of stay of two days. This suggests that the differences in total costs between hospitals are related to something other than length of stay. Possible explanations for these differences are hospital size and services provided.

Analysis Implications

The exploratory analysis presented in this case illustrates the use of visualization to become familiar with the variability of each data element, examine outliers, identify variables that are not candidates for further analysis (at least initially), and view relationships between variables. Such exploratory analysis is indispensable at the beginning of an inquiry and forms the foundation for subsequent analyses.

In data sets with more than a few variables, the number of possible combinations of variables is very large and considerable time and resources may be needed to examine a large number of combinations. An understanding of the problem domain in conjunction with insight gained from basic descriptive analysis can guide the development of an analysis strategy that will meet the needs of stakeholders. Gaining deeper understanding through consulting subject matter experts and pertinent references helps in selecting and interpreting meaningful analyses.

With large data sets, such as are available from SPARCS. significance testing is often of little value, as very small differences will be statistically significant, but not of practical significance. In the next two cases, we will continue our analysis of the Adirondack newborns data by developing predictive models through regression analysis.

Data Definitions

The data definitions can be found in "Inpatient Hospital Discharges (SPARCS De-Identified File): CY 2014 DATA DICTIONARY," which is located in the JMP project ADK_Newborns_2014.jmpprj.

Problems

1 Perform additional analysis on the individual variables in this case.

   a Examine the outlier with a birthweight of 7500 g. What additional information would be helpful to have to disposition this outlier? Would you exclude this outlier from further analysis? Justify your decision.

   b Identify variables in the data set that you think would not be useful in the analysis of total cost. Explain your rationale.

   c Examine the distributions for Admit Day of the Week and Discharge Day of the Week. Do these distributions seem reasonable? Explain why or why not.

2 Analyze total costs graphically for possible relationships with gender and CCS Procedure Aggregated. Discuss your findings and compare them to those presented in this case.

3 What other factors, not contained in the data set for this case, might explain the differences in total costs between the eight hospitals? Review the websites of these hospitals and collect additional data. Create data visualizations to help determine if these factors are related to total costs. (Hint: consider the number of beds.)

4 Select another region of New York State and download the data for newborns from SPARCS for 2014. Repeat the analysis of this case and compare your results to those of the Adirondack region.

Reference

CDC Growth Charts, Weight-for-age percentiles, Girls birth to 36 months, https://www.cdc.gov/growthcharts/data/set1/chart02.pdf, accessed June 4, 2017.

12

Building a Simple Predictive Model for Health Care Costs for Newborns in Adirondack Hospitals

Chapter Summary Concepts

Statistical Concepts	Data Management Concepts	JMP Features
Data visualization • Histogram • Scatterplot • Residual plot	Subsetting data	Rows > Data Filter
Descriptive statistics	Derived data	Tables > Subset
Simple linear regression	Units conversion	Distribution
		Tabulate
		Fit Y by X
		Lasso tool

Background

The Adirondack region of New York State is dominated by the Adirondack Park, 6.1 million acres of both publically and privately owned land designated as "forever wild." Closely regulated land use and development, rugged terrain, and low population density contribute in part to limited employment opportunities, poverty, an aging population, and a shortage of health care providers. Primary care and specialty physicians and home health care aides are in short supply in many Adirondack counties. Governmental and non-profit organizations have initiated a number of programs to improve access to health care including expanded programs to train health care workers at regional colleges and universities, school loan forgiveness programs to attract physicians to work in rural areas, and services to obtain affordable insurance. Periodically, the New York State Board of Regents publishes a listing of those counties and hospitals that are experiencing shortages of various types of health care providers.

In the case "Health Care Costs for Newborns in Adirondack Hospitals" we conducted an exploratory data analysis of inpatient hospital stays for newborns in the Adirondack region of New York. The goal was to identify factors that were potential predictors of the total costs associated with the newborn hospital stays. In this case, we will look at newborn data for the Champlain Valley Physicians Hospital, located in Clinton County that was designated in 2013 as having both primary and non-primary care shortages.

Problem Statement

For infants born at the Champlain Valley Physicians Hospital (CVPH) in 2014:

- What is the relationship between total costs and length of stay?
- What is the relationship between total costs and birth weight?

The Data

A subset of the data from the case "Health Care Costs for Newborns in Adirondack Hospitals" will be used in this case. The data source is New York State's Statewide Planning and Research Cooperative System (SPARCS) which collects patient-level health care data for the purpose of providing health care organizations with information that will enable them to efficiently and cost effectively deliver services. This data reporting system was established in 1979 and collects data on patient characteristics, diagnoses, treatments, and services for inpatient, ambulatory surgery, emergency department admission, and outpatient visits. We will use the publically available, de-identified data for inpatient stays for 2014 to examine the total costs associated with newborns. Total costs are the actual cost of the services provided; total charges are the amounts charged to insurers.

Data Management

Creating a Data Subset

Open the file ADK_Newborns_2014.jmp and select Rows > Data Filter. Add the column Facility Name and from the resulting dialog highlight Champlain Valley Physicians Hospital as shown in Figure 12.1 on page 188.

Figure 12.1 *Data Filter to Select Subset*

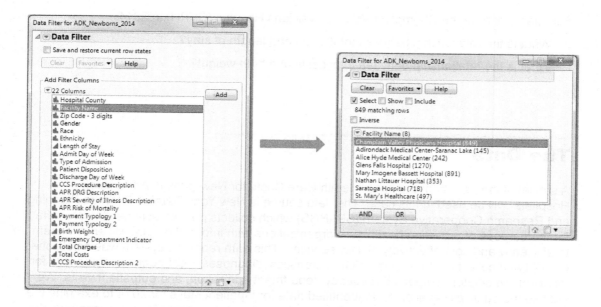

All records corresponding to the Champlain Valley Physicians Hospital will be selected in the JMP data table. To create a new data table containing only these records select Tables > Subset and from the resulting dialog choose the radio button for Selected Rows. The new data table is renamed to CVPH_Newborns_2014.jmp using File > Save as. The file is now ready for analysis.

Creating Derived Data

In SPARCS, birthweight is recorded in grams. This scale of measurement is not commonly used by the general public to describe birthweight. To facilitate comprehension of the variation in birthweight we will create a column that expresses birthweight in pounds. Create a new column, right click over the column heading and select Formula. Figure 12.2 on page 189 shows the Formula Editor containing the equation that will convert grams to pounds.

Figure 12.2   *Formula Editor Showing Equation to Convert Grams to Pounds*

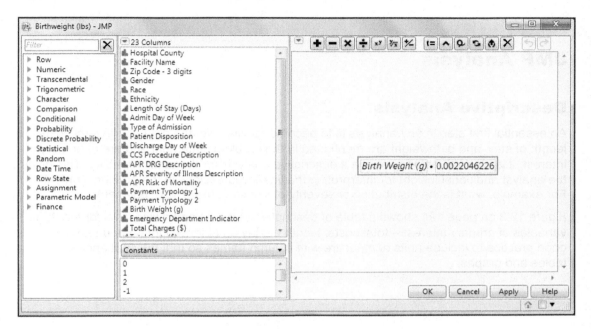

Analytic Approach

The three questions below will guide the selection of appropriate methods to quantify the relationship between total costs and length of stay and total costs and birthweight.

1   What is the response (Y) of interest and how is it measured? Total costs is the response variable found in the problem statement. It is a continuous variable.

2   Are predictor variables mentioned in the problem statement? If so, how many and what are their measurement levels? The problem statement gives two separate research questions, each specifies one predictor of total costs, length of stay and birthweight, respectively. Both of these predictor variables are continuous.

3   What are you being asked to deliver? A data description, an interval estimate, an answer to a question, or a predictive model? You are being asked to quantify the relationship between total costs and length of stay and total costs and birthweight. A predictive equation will quantify these relationships. A simple linear regression is a good starting point for developing a predictive equation. Evaluating the linear model may suggest the need for a more complicated model (e.g., non-linear or multivariable).

JMP Analysis

Descriptive Analysis

An essential first step in any analysis is to become familiar with the data. While total costs, length of stay, and birthweight are mentioned in the problem statement and are of primary interest, it is also valuable to provide a descriptive analysis for the other variables. This gives the analyst additional insight for interpreting the linear regressions in the problem context. For example, what is the distribution of severity of illness or the type of payment?

Figure 12.3 on page 191 shows a table of descriptive statistics and histograms for the three variables of primary interest – total costs, length of stay and birthweight (in pounds). It is good practice to include units of measure with column names so that they will appear in tables and graphs.

Figure 12.3 *Descriptive Analysis for Total Costs, Length of Stay, and Birthweight*

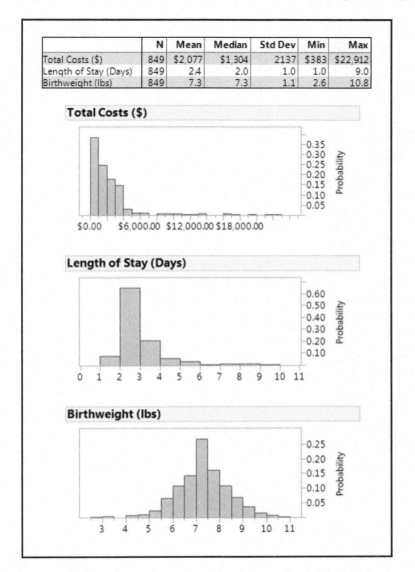

	N	Mean	Median	Std Dev	Min	Max
Total Costs ($)	849	$2,077	$1,304	2137	$383	$22,912
Length of Stay (Days)	849	2.4	2.0	1.0	1.0	9.0
Birthweight (lbs)	849	7.3	7.3	1.1	2.6	10.8

Figure 12.4 on page 192 shows descriptive statistics for the other variables in the data set. These tables were created with the Tabulate function with the variables grouped by categories such as demographics, admission, diagnosis, and payment.

Figure 12.4 *Descriptive Statistics for Other Variables*

Tabulate

Gender	N	% of Total
F	407	47.9%
M	442	52.1%
Race		
Black/African American	12	1.4%
Other Race	222	26.1%
White	615	72.4%
Ethnicity		
Not Span/Hispanic	846	99.6%
Spanish/Hispanic	3	0.4%
Emergency Department Indicator		
N	849	100.0%
Admit Day of Week		
SUN	58	6.8%
MON	125	14.7%
TUE	158	18.6%
WED	164	19.3%
THU	148	17.4%
FRI	121	14.3%
SAT	75	8.8%
Discharge Day of Week		
SUN	129	15.2%
MON	89	10.5%
TUE	62	7.3%
WED	112	13.2%
THU	146	17.2%
FRI	171	20.1%
SAT	140	16.5%

Tabulate

APR DRG Description	N	% of Total
NEONATE BIRTHWT >2499G W CONGENITAL/PERINATAL INFECTION	7	0.8%
NEONATE BIRTHWT >2499G W MAJOR ANOMALY	7	0.8%
NEONATE BIRTHWT >2499G W OTHER SIGNIFICANT CONDITION	7	0.8%
NEONATE BIRTHWT >2499G, NORMAL NEWBORN OR NEONATE W OTHER PROBLEM	787	92.7%
NEONATE BWT <500G	1	0.1%
NEONATE BWT 2000-2499G, NORMAL NEWBORN OR NEONATE W OTHER PROBLEM	26	3.1%
NEONATE, BIRTHWT >2499G W RESP DIST SYND/OTH MAJ RESP COND	1	0.1%
NEONATE, TRANSFERRED < 5 DAYS OLD, BORN HERE	13	1.5%
CCS Procedure Description		
CIRCUMCISION	312	36.7%
DIAGNOSTIC SPINAL TAP	2	0.2%
NO PROC	43	5.1%
OPHTHALM-/OT-OLOGIC DX	10	1.2%
OT NON-OR THER PRC SKIN	2	0.2%
OT VASC CATH; NOT HEART	1	0.1%
OTHER THERAPEUTIC PRCS	25	2.9%
PROPHYLACTIC VAC/INOCUL	450	53.0%
RESP INTUB/MECH VENTIL	4	0.5%
APR Severity of Illness Description		
Minor	755	88.9%
Moderate	80	9.4%
Major	13	1.5%
Extreme	1	0.1%
APR Severity of Illness Description		
Minor	755	88.9%
Moderate	80	9.4%
Major	13	1.5%
Extreme	1	0.1%
APR Risk of Mortality		
Minor	845	99.5%
Moderate	1	0.1%
Major	1	0.1%
Extreme	2	0.2%

Tabulate

Payment Typology 1	N	% of Total
Blue Cross/Blue Shield	314	37.0%
Federal/State/Local/VA	13	1.5%
Medicaid	310	36.5%
Medicare	4	0.5%
Private Health Insurance	163	19.2%
Self-Pay	39	4.6%
Unknown	6	0.7%
Payment Typology 2		
Blue Cross/Blue Shield	3	17.6%
Federal/State/Local/VA	2	11.8%
Medicaid	6	35.3%
Private Health Insurance	2	11.8%
Self-Pay	4	23.5%

For some variables, all observations have the same value. In some cases this is due to the subset being analyzed (e.g., the Hospital County is Clinton for all observations since we are only looking at one hospital). In other cases, such as Emergency Department Indicator, variation is possible but for CVPH in 2014 no newborns were admitted through the Emergency Department. It is tempting to omit the description of Emergency Department Indicator because there is no variation, but including this information adds insight in the problem context.

Simple Regression Analysis: Total Costs and Length of Stay

Fitting the Regression Model

A good practice prior to developing a bivariate predictive model is to visualize the relationship on a scatterplot. From the Analyze menu select the Fit Y by X platform and enter Total Costs in the Y, Response field and Length of Stay in the X, Factor field. The resulting scatterplot is shown in Figure 12.5 on page 193.

Figure 12.5 *Scatterplot of Total Costs and Length of Stay*

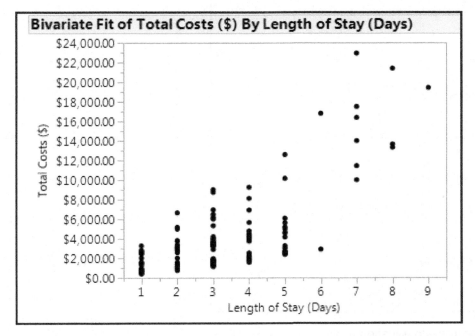

As expected, as length of stay increases, total costs increase. The correlation between Total Costs and Length of Stay is 0.66 as found in the correlation matrix obtained by selecting

Analysis > Multivariate Methods > Multivariate. A simple linear regression analysis will model this relationship as a straight line and allow us to quantify the relationship. It is good practice to start with a simple model, assess the adequacy of the model, and if necessary proceed to developing more complex models.

To find the best fitting line select Fit Line from the drop-down menu. The fitted line and data are shown graphically in Figure 12.6 on page 194 along with the associated numerical output.

Figure 12.6 *Linear Fit for Total Costs and Length of Stay*

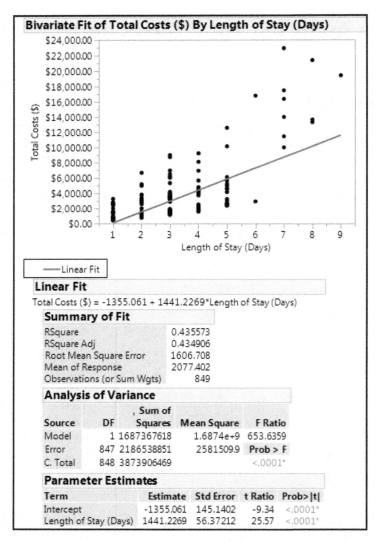

The estimated regression equation is:

Total Costs = -1355.061 + 1441.227*Length of Stay

This best fit line is found using the ordinary least squares method where the estimated slope and intercept are chosen to minimize the sum of the squared distances from the observations to the fitted line. The intercept of -1355.06 is the estimated average total cost when length of stay is zero. Since it does not make sense to have an inpatient hospital stay of 0 days, the intercept is not interpreted in the problem context, but serves as a fitting constant. The slope indicates that for each increase of one day in length of stay there is an estimated average increase of $1441.23 in total costs. The slope is an estimate of the daily cost of hospitalization for newborns. Always assess the slope coefficient for reasonableness in the problem context. Do both the sign and magnitude make sense? The slope is positive which says that as length of stay goes up total costs go up. A quick internet search for average daily hospital costs will assist in determining the reasonableness of the magnitude of the slope. It appears that $1441.23 is a plausible daily charge.

To establish if length of stay is a significant predictor of total costs, a test of hypothesis should be conducted for the slope coefficient. The Parameter Estimates table in Figure 12.6 on page 194 shows the t-ratio and p-value (Prob > |t|) associated with a test of hypothesis that the slope is equal to zero versus the alternative that the slope is different from zero. The p-value is <0.0001 which indicates that length of stay is a significant predictor of total costs for infants born in Champlain Valley Physicians Hospital in 2014.

Assessing the Model Fit

Once the regression line is determined to be significant, an assessment of the goodness-of-fit of the model to the data is warranted. The coefficient of determination, R^2, is a measure of goodness-of-fit and gives the proportion of the variation in total costs explained by length of stay. This is found in the JMP output of Figure 12.6 on page 194 in the Summary of Fit table. The Rsquare is 0.44 for this simple linear regression. There is no general rule of thumb for what constitutes a good R^2, but since it is unitless it is useful for comparing different models. R^2 is sensitive to outliers and the range of the independent variable.

The root mean squared error (RMSE) is the standard deviation about the regression line. The RMSE is in the units of the dependent variable and can be found in the Summary of Fit table in Figure 12.6 on page 194. Comparing the RMSE to the standard deviation of the dependent variable is useful in assessing the goodness-of-fit of the linear regression. A RMSE that is less than the standard deviation of the dependent variable (total costs) indicates that the model has explained some of the variability in the dependent variable. For the CVPH regression the RMSE is $1607 and the standard deviation of total costs (see Figure 12.3 on page 191) is $2137, which indicates the linear regression has explained some of the variability in total cost.

Assessing the RMSE in the problem context helps determine if the model is adequate for prediction. For example, a RMSE on the order of tens of dollars would indicate that the model is useful for predicting total costs associated with childbirth while a RMSE on the order of thousands of dollars is not sufficiently precise to be of much practical value.

Finally, assess the line fit visually. In the scatterplot shown in Figure 12.6 on page 194 we see that the line underestimates total costs for longer lengths of stay. Intuitively, we would expect longer lengths of stay for a newborn when there are complications. The JMP Lasso tool allows groups of points to be selected by "drawing" a region on a JMP graph. Some of the longer length of stay observations have been selected from the scatterplot using the Lasso tool as shown in Figure 12.7 on page 196. This will allow to us look for patterns in other variables that may help explain why the model underestimates total costs for these observations.

Figure 12.7   *Longer Length of Stay Observations Selected with the Lasso Tool*

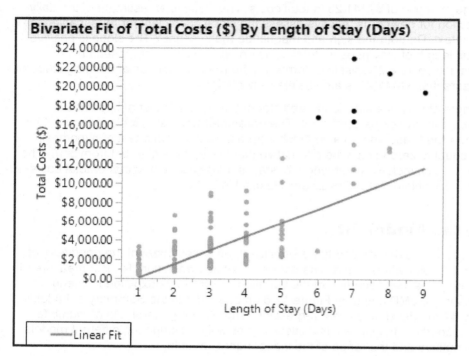

The selected observations appear darker than those that are not selected. The corresponding rows in the JMP data table are highlighted and by applying Table > Subset a new data table can be created to facilitate examination of other variables. Most of these newborns had complications such as infections or respiratory conditions.

Assessing Regression Assumptions with Residual Plots

Evaluating the regression equation at a given length of stay yields a predicted total cost. For example, the predicted total cost for a five day length of stay is $5851.07. The difference between an observed and predicted value at a given length of stay is referred to as a residual. Residuals capture the variation in total cost that is not explained by the linear model. Plotting residuals allows the analyst to assess the regression model fit and to verify regression assumptions.

To obtain residual plots select Plot Residuals from the Linear Fit drop-down menu as shown in Figure 12.8 on page 197.

Figure 12.8 *Requesting Residual Plots from Fit Y by X Linear Fit*

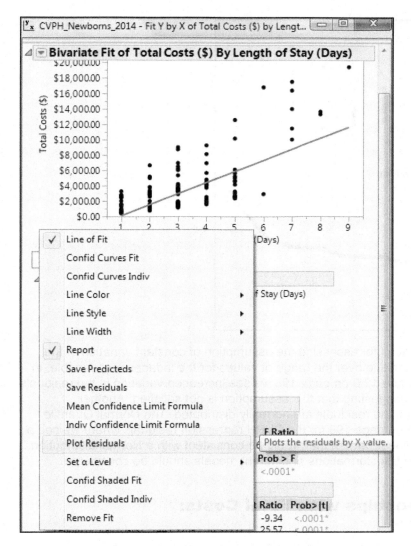

Figure 12.9 on page 198 shows two of the resulting residual plots that assist in assessing regression assumptions.

Figure 12.9 *Selected Residual Plots*

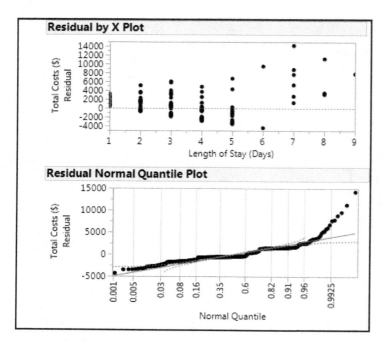

The Residual by X Plot is useful for assessing the assumption of constant variation of the residuals about the regression line over the range of values for the independent variable. In the Residual by X Plot in Figure 12.9 on page 198 we see increased variation in the residuals as length of stay increases suggesting that this assumption is not satisfied. Another regression assumption is that the residuals are normally distributed. The Normal Quantile plot is shown in Figure 12.9 on page 198 for the CVPH regression residuals where we see a serious departure from the linear pattern that would be consistent with a Normal distribution. In light of these issues, data transformations or different models should be considered.

Exploring Relationships with Total Costs: Birthweight

Repeating the simple regression process with birthweight (in pounds) as the independent variable will address the second research question posed in the problem statement. The results are shown in Figure 12.10 on page 199.

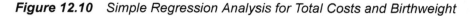

Figure 12.10 *Simple Regression Analysis for Total Costs and Birthweight*

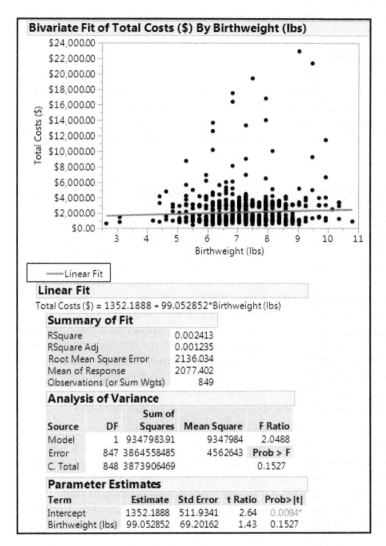

Bivariate Fit of Total Costs ($) By Birthweight (lbs)

── Linear Fit

Linear Fit

Total Costs ($) = 1352.1888 + 99.052852*Birthweight (lbs)

Summary of Fit

RSquare	0.002413
RSquare Adj	0.001235
Root Mean Square Error	2136.034
Mean of Response	2077.402
Observations (or Sum Wgts)	849

Analysis of Variance

Source	DF	Sum of Squares	Mean Square	F Ratio
Model	1	9347983.91	9347984	2.0488
Error	847	3864558485	4562643	Prob > F
C. Total	848	3873906469		0.1527

Parameter Estimates

Term	Estimate	Std Error	t Ratio	Prob>|t|
Intercept	1352.1888	511.9341	2.64	0.0084*
Birthweight (lbs)	99.052852	69.20162	1.43	0.1527

The fitted line has a very shallow slope and there is considerable scatter about the regression line. The slope coefficient quantifies that linear relationship as an increase of one pound in birthweight results in an estimated average increase in total costs of $99.05. However, the slope coefficient is not significantly different from zero (using a 5% significance level) since the p-value (Prob > |t| from the Parameter Estimates table) is 0.1527. The means that birthweight is not a significant predictor of total costs. When the test of hypothesis for the slope is not significant, no further analysis, such as assessing goodness-of-fit, should be conducted.

Analysis Implications

Simple regression revealed that taken alone length of stay is a significant predictor of total costs. However, the linear model underestimates the total costs associated with longer lengths of stay. It makes sense that the longer a newborn stays in the hospital, the higher the total costs, but this does not tell the whole story. Additional costs are likely incurred that are related to the various diagnoses and there will be different costs associated with the type and quantity of treatments.

Birthweight was shown not to be a significant predictor of total costs. This contradicts our expectations as low birthweight is usually associated with premature birth and the resulting complications require additional therapies and hence increased costs. However, there is no information given in the data set that indicates if the births were premature. The de-identified data is inherently restricted in the details provided to maintain patient anonymity. This may limit the ability to create an adequate predictive model. The full SPARCS data contains additional information that may result in a better predictive model. The limitations of the data set used should always be considered when determining if the statistical model adequately addresses the problem posed. Reviewing the services offered at the Champlain Valley Physicians Hospital (New York State Department of Health website) shows that the hospital is designated as a Level 1 Perinatal Center which only provides care for normal and low-risk deliveries and does not have a neonatal intensive care unit. Since premature infants are often low birth weight, it seems reasonable that such infants born at CVPH would be transferred to another hospital having more neonatal care services. Conducting such additional research can often help explain the reasonableness of statistical results.

A good strategy for attacking a statistical problem is to begin simply and proceed to more complicated models. Descriptive, univariate analysis is a crucial first step to become familiar with the data. This is followed by bivariate and then multivariate analysis. At each stage, a better understanding of the data and the relationships between variables is obtained which guides subsequent, more complicated analyses. As a next step, a multiple regression analysis would create a predictive equation for total costs with multiple independent variables and may have improved explanatory power.

Data Definitions

The data definitions can be found in *Inpatient Hospital Discharges (SPARCS De-Identified File): CY 2014 DATA DICTIONARY* which is located in the JMP project ADK_Newborns_2014.jmpprj.

The definitions of the derived data are given in the table below.

Data Element	Description
CCS Procedure Aggregated	Derived from CCS Procedure Description where less common procedures are aggregated into a single category, "OTHER PRCS"
Birthweight (lbs)	Newborn birthweight expressed in pounds

Problems

1 Analyze the 2014 newborn data for the Alice Hyde Medical Center, located in the Capital/ Adirondack health service area.

    a Create a new JMP data table for the Alice Hyde Medical Center data.

    b Perform simple linear regression analyses to predict total costs from length of stay and total costs from birthweight.

    c Compare your results with those found in this case for the Champlain Valley Physicians Hospital.

    d Conduct research to characterize differences between these two hospitals and the communities that they serve. How do they differ? How might these differences affect the results of your analysis?

2 Based on the results from this case study, length of stay alone seems insufficient to fully explain the total hospital costs associated with newborns. Repeat the steps to produce the simple regression that predicts total costs from length of stay. Then use Rows > Color or Mark by Column and select another variable that may help explain the disproportionately high costs for the longer length of stays. Examine the regression plot. Are there colors patterns that suggest this variable is a possible predictor of total costs?

3 Select another New York State hospital outside of the Capital/Adirondack health service area and download the data for newborns from SPARCS for 2014. Repeat the analysis of this case and compare your results to those of Champlain Valley Physicians Hospital.

Reference

"REGENTS DESIGNATED PHYSICIAN SHORTAGE AREAS In NEW YORK STATE," January 1, 2013, http://www.highered.nysed.gov/kiap/precoll/documents/ 2013ShortageBulletin.pdf, accessed June 18, 2017.

13

Building a Multivariate Predictive Model for Health Care Costs for Newborns in Adirondack Hospitals

Chapter Summary Concepts

Statistical Concepts	Data Management Concepts	JMP Features
Data visualization		Multivariate
• Scatterplot		
• Residual plot		
Simple correlation analysis		Distribution
Simple linear regression		Fit Y by X
Multiple linear regression		Fit Model

Background

In 2008, New York State enacted the Doctors Across New York program to improve health care access in rural communities by offering incentives to attract and retain physicians in underserved regions. Initiatives associated with this program include financial support to join or establish a practice, recruiting physicians to underserved hospitals, and physician educational loan repayment.

The Adirondack region of New York State is experiencing physician shortages. In 2013 the Champlain Valley Physicians Hospital (CVPH), located in Plattsburgh, was designated by the state Board of Regents as having shortages of both primary and non-primary care physicians. CVPH is a member of the University of Vermont Health Network which is comprised of six hospitals serving northern New York and Vermont. It has 300 inpatient beds, 21 maternity beds, and is a Level 1 perinatal center. A Level 1 perinatal center does not have a neonatal intensive care unit and handles only normal and low-risk deliveries. Plattsburgh is the largest city in northeastern New York with a population of approximately 32,000 in the immediate area. It is situated on the western shore of Lake Champlain and is in close proximity to Montreal, Quebec. Major employers are in the higher education and transportation industries.

This case continues our exploration of predictors of the total costs associated with inpatient newborn stays begun in the cases "Health Care Costs for Newborns in Adirondack Hospitals" and "Building a Simple Predictive Model for Health Care Costs for Newborns in Adirondack Hospitals."

Problem Statement

For infants born at the Champlain Valley Physicians Hospital in 2014 do length of stay and birthweight together predict total costs?

The Data

This case will analyze the same data set that was used in ""Building a Simple Predictive Model for Health Care Costs for Newborns in Adirondack Hospitals." The data can be found in the file CVPH_Newborn_2014.jmp. The data source is New York State's Statewide Planning and Research Cooperative System (SPARCS) which collects patient level health care data for the purpose of providing health care organizations with information that will enable them to efficiently and cost effectively deliver services. We will use the publicly available, de-identified data for inpatient stays for 2014 to examine the total cost associated with newborns. Total costs refer to the actual cost of the services provided.

Data Management

No additional data processing is required for CVPH_Newborn_2014.jmp.

Analytic Approach

The three questions below will guide the selection of appropriate methods to quantify the relationship between total costs and length of stay and birthweight.

1 What is the response (Y) of interest and how is it measured? Total costs is the response variable found in the problem statement. It is a continuous variable.

2 Are predictor variables mentioned in the problem statement? If so, how many and what are their measurement levels? The problem statement requests a simultaneous prediction of total costs from length of stay and birthweight. Both of these predictor variables are continuous.

3 What are you being asked to deliver? A data description, an interval estimate, an answer to a question, or a predictive model? You are being asked to quantify the relationship between total costs and length of stay and birthweight. A predictive equation will quantify this relationship. A multiple linear regression is a good starting point for developing a predictive equation. Multiple regression is a flexible modeling method to predict a continuous variable from nominal, ordinal, or continuous independent variables.

JMP Analysis

Descriptive Analysis

A univariate descriptive analysis for the variables in the data set appears in the case "Building a Simple Predictive Model for Health Care Costs for Newborns in Adirondack Hospitals." When conducting a multiple regression, a simple correlation analysis is a useful preparatory step that can help identify independent variables that may be good predictors and independent variables that are highly correlated. Including highly correlated independent variables in a multiple regression can be problematic as will be discussed subsequently.

The Pearson correlation coefficient describes the degree of linear association between two continuous variables. Correlation is measured on a scale of -1 to 1 where -1 represents a perfect inverse relationship, 0 represents no relationship, and 1 represents a perfect direct relationship. There are three continuous variables of interest in the data set: total costs, length of stay, and birthweight (lbs). To compute the correlation between all pairs, select Analyze > Multivariate Methods > Multivariate. From the drop-down menu choose Pairwise Correlations. The results are shown in Figure 13.1 on page 207.

Figure 13.1 *Correlation Analysis*

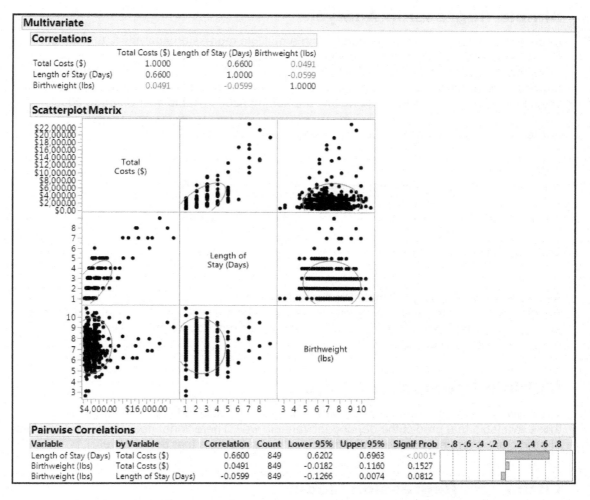

The correlation matrix shows the estimated correlation coefficients for each pair of variables. The matrix is symmetric about the diagonal. The Scatterplot Matrix shows scatterplots for each pair of variables. These graphs are useful to identify outliers. The Pairwise Correlation table shows the estimated correlation coefficient, 95% confidence bounds, and the p-value (Signif Prob) associated with the test of hypothesis that the correlation is zero (meaning no linear association) against an alternative that the correlation is not equal to zero (meaning significant linear association).

Total Costs and Length of Stay have a significant correlation of 0.66. The correlation between Total Costs and Birthweight (lbs) is not significant. The correlation between Birthweight (lbs) and Length of Stay is not significant at the 5% level. The low correlation suggests that including both of these predictors in a multiple regression will not be problematic.

Simple Regression Analysis

Another preparatory step prior to conducting a multiple regression analysis is to examine simple regression results for key independent variables. In the case "Building a Simple Predictive Model for Health Care Costs for Newborns in Adirondack Hospitals," simple regression analysis found that taken alone, length of stay was a significant predictor of total costs but birthweight was not. The results are summarized in Table 13.1 on page 208.

Table 13.1 *Summary of Simple Regression Analysis for Total Costs*

Independent Variable	Slope Significance	R^2	RMSE
Length of stay	<0.0001	0.44	$1607
Birthweight (lbs)	0.1527	0.002	$2136

As discussed in "Building a Simple Predictive Model for Health Care Costs for Newborns in Adirondack Hospitals," while the length of stay is a significant predictor of total costs, there are likely other factors that influence total cost such as procedures and treatments associated with birth complications.

Multiple Regression Analysis

The objective of multiple regression analysis is to find a set of independent variables from those available that predict the dependent variable well. There is not necessarily one best set of predictors; there may be several different sets of predictors that perform well.

Fitting the Regression Model

Since birthweight alone is not a significant predictor of total costs, it is tempting to not include it in a multiple regression model. But to satisfy the problem statement, we will construct a multiple regression equation with length of stay and birthweight (lbs) as predictors.

From the JMP menu select Analyze > Fit Model and enter the variables Total Costs ($), Length of Stay (Days), and Birthweight (lbs) as shown in Figure 13.2 on page 209.

Figure 13.2 *Fit Model Dialog for Multiple Regression*

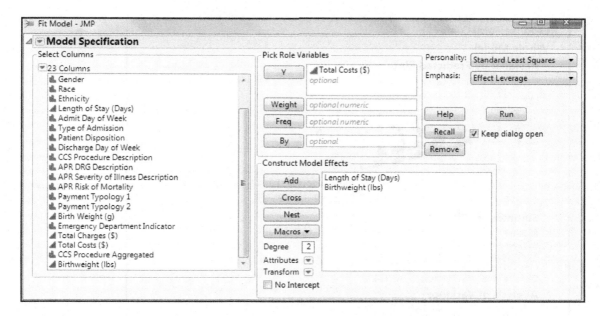

Be sure and check "Keep dialog open." This makes it easy to change predictors in the regression. The basic multiple regression output is shown in Figure 13.3 on page 210. From this output, the Regression Reports option can be invoked from the drop-down menu to select output to display. Non-essential portions of the output have been hidden using the gray toggles at the left of each table or graph.

Figure 13.3 *Basic Multiple Regression Results from Fit Model*

Response Total Costs ($)

Whole Model

Residual by Predicted Plot

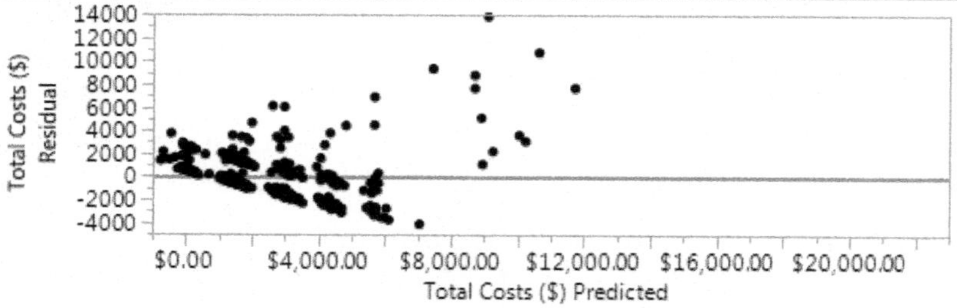

Summary of Fit

RSquare	0.443458
RSquare Adj	0.442142
Root Mean Square Error	1596.388
Mean of Response	2077.402
Observations (or Sum Wgts)	849

Analysis of Variance

Source	DF	Sum of Squares	Mean Square	F Ratio
Model	2	1717913660	858956830	337.0500
Error	846	2155992809	2548454.9	Prob > F
C. Total	848	3873906469		<.0001*

Parameter Estimates

Term	Estimate	Std Error	t Ratio	Prob>|t|
Intercept	-2696.062	413.3119	-6.52	<.0001*
Length of Stay (Days)	1452.8581	56.11072	25.89	<.0001*
Birthweight (lbs)	179.37641	51.81152	3.46	0.0006*

The Parameter Estimates table gives the regression coefficients and the t Ratio and p-value (Prob>|t|) associated with the significance tests. The estimated multiple regression equation is:

Total Costs = -2696.06 + 1425.86Length of Stay + 179.38Birthweight (lbs).

The interpretation of the regression coefficients are:

- When Length of Stay and Birthweight (lbs) are zero, the estimated average Total Costs are -$2696.06. Clearly, such an observation is not possible and the intercept serves as a fitting constant for the model.

- For each increase in one day of hospitalization there is an estimated average increase of $1425.86 in total cost holding birthweight constant.

- For each increase in one pound of birthweight, there is an estimated average increase of $179.38 in total cost holding length of stay constant.

As with simple linear regression, the method of least squares is used to obtain the regression coefficients.

The Parameter Estimates table shows the significance test of each regression coefficient with the null hypothesis is that the regression coefficient is equal to zero against the alternative that the regression coefficient is not equal to zero. Both length of stay and birthweight are significant predictors (at the 5% level) of total costs since the p-values associated with the significance tests for the regression coefficients are less than 0.05. The significance of a predictor in a multiple regression equation depends on the other predictors in the equation. While birthweight was not significant as a predictor of total costs in a simple regression, it is significant in a multiple regression that includes length of stay. For this reason, independent variables should be added or removed one at a time as you seek a good predictive equation. The goal is to have a multiple regression that includes only significant predictors of the dependent variable. However, there are special circumstances where non-significant variables should be included, such as when required by a regulatory agency.

To predict the total costs for specific values of length of stay and birthweight, the values are substituted into the regression equation. For example, a two day hospital stay for a seven pound newborn would have a predicted total cost of $1411.32. Predictions can be made from the estimated regression in JMP by selecting Save Columns > Prediction Formula from the drop-down menu. This will create a new column in the JMP data table that contains the formula for the regression equation. Add a new row to the data table, fill in the desired values for the predictors and the predicted value of total costs will appear in the new column. Evaluating a regression model for values of the independent variables beyond the observed ranges is referred to as extrapolation and is not recommended. We do not know if the relationships between the dependent and independent variables estimated by the regression equation are valid outside of the observed ranges.

Assessing the Model Fit – R^2 and RMSE

Similar to simple regression, R^2 and the RMSE are used to assess the adequacy of the model fit. The R^2 and RMSE can be found in the Summary of Fit table shown in Figure 13.3 on page 210. Table 13.2 on page 211 summarizes the goodness-of-fit measures for the two simple regressions and the multiple regression containing both length of stay and birthweight.

Table 13.2 *Comparison of Simple Regressions and a Two-Variable Multiple Regression*

Independent Variables	Slope Significance	R^2	RMSE
Length of stay	<0.0001	0.436	$1607
Birthweight (lbs)	0.1527	0.002	$2136
Length of Stay	<0.0001	0.443	$1596
Birthweight (lbs)	0.0006		

While both length of stay and birthweight are significant in the multiple regression, there is only slight improvement in the R^2 and RMSE compared to the simple regression with length of stay.

Assessing the Model Fit – Multicollinearity

An additional concern in multiple regression is multicollinearity, which occurs when there are highly correlated independent variables in a regression equation. This can affect regression coefficients causing them to have the wrong sign, have decreased precision, or have very different magnitudes depending on the other variables in the model. Examining pairwise correlations can suggest such highly correlated predictors, however there are situations where multicollinearity is not revealed through the correlation coefficients. Variance Inflation Factors (VIF) are used to diagnose multicollinearity. To obtain the VIFs, right click anywhere in the Parameter Estimates table and from the resulting menu select Columns > VIF as shown in Figure 13.4 on page 212.

Figure 13.4 *Dialog to Request Variance Inflation Factors*

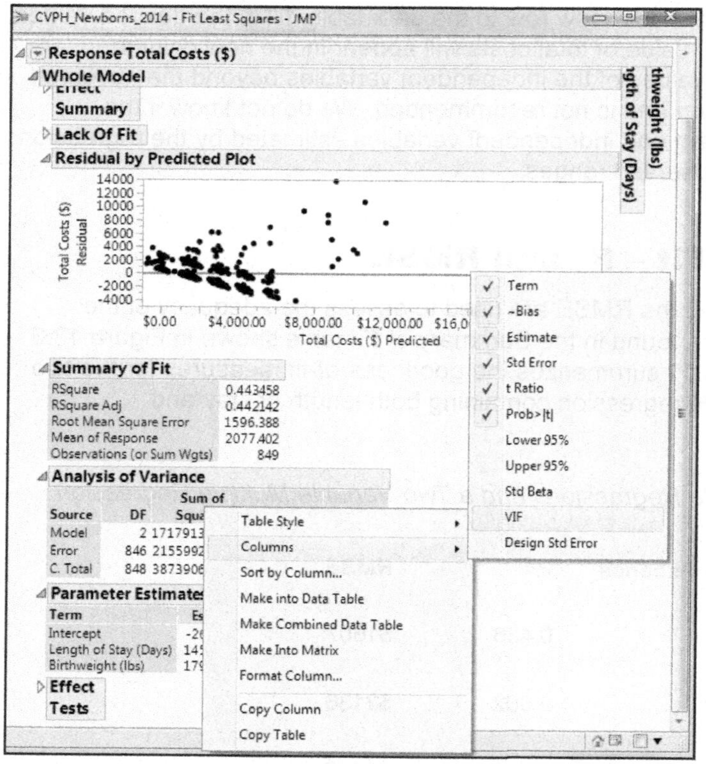

The Parameter Estimates table is expanded to include the VIFs as shown in Figure 13.5 on page 213.

Figure 13.5 *Parameter Estimates Table with Variance Inflation Factors*

Response Total Costs ($)					
Whole Model					
Parameter Estimates					
Term	Estimate	Std Error	t Ratio	Prob>|t|	VIF
Intercept	-2696.062	413.3119	-6.52	<.0001*	.
Length of Stay (Days)	1452.8581	56.11072	25.89	<.0001*	1.0035978
Birthweight (lbs)	179.37641	51.81152	3.46	0.0006*	1.0035978

The following are general guidelines for interpreting VIFs. When a VIF is a less than five, there is no cause for concern. When the VIF ranges from 5 to 10, there is potential for multicollinearity; and a VIF greater than 10 means there is multicollinearity in the model. When VIFs are greater than five, the analyst should remove one of the correlated variables and assess the effect on the regression coefficients and the goodness-of-fit measures. In this example, both VIFs are less than five and hence there is no concern with multicollinearity.

Assessing the Model Fit with Residual Plots

Residual plots are used to assess the goodness-of-fit of the multiple regression. A multiple regression with two predictors can be visualized as a plane and a three dimensional plot allows comparison of the observations to the regression plane. When there are more than two predictors, the model cannot be visualized. Residual plots are used instead to visually assess the model fit. Patterns observed in the residual plots suggest a systematic effect that should be included in the model as either additional predictors or non-linear terms. Patterns of randomly scatter residuals are indicative of a good model fit.

The Fit Model platform offers an option to save the residuals to a new column in the data table as shown in Figure 13.6 on page 214. This will allow a variety of residual plots to be created.

Figure 13.6 *Dialog to Request Residuals to be Saved to Data Table*

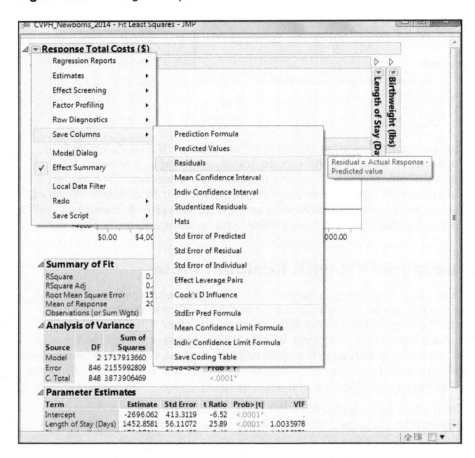

Figure 13.7 on page 215 shows one of the default residual plots that can be obtained from the drop-down menu by selecting Row Diagnostics > Plot Residual by Predicted.

Figure 13.7 *Residual Plot for Multiple Regression*

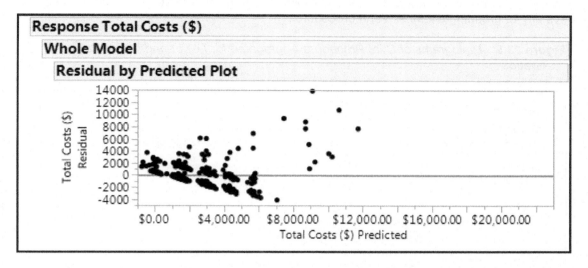

In this plot we see three groupings. Two groups show decreasing residuals as predicted total costs increase. The third group has positive residuals at higher predicted total costs, meaning that the multiple regression underestimates higher total costs when they are higher. This pattern did not emerge in the comparable residual plot for the simple linear regression with length of stay as the predictor which is shown in Figure 13.8 on page 215 as obtained from the Fit Y by X platform.

Figure 13.8 *Residual Plot for Simple Linear Regression with Length of Stay*

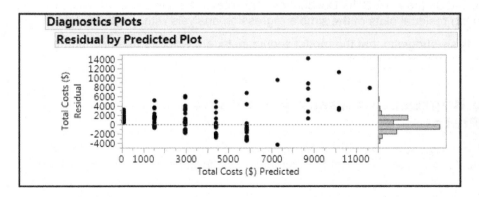

Notice that in the simple regression length of stay is integer and as such there will be limited number of predicted values. This is not the case in the multiple regression.

The residual groupings in Figure 13.7 on page 215 suggest additional effects are present that are not included in the model. When a good-fitting model is obtained, residual plots will show a random scatter, free of noticeable patterns. To better understand these groupings, we will use the lasso tool to select groups, create individual data tables and then examine other variables in these groups using the Distribution platform. For example, Figure 13.9 on page

216 shows the histograms of CCS Procedure Aggregated for the lower and upper groups of linearly decreasing residuals. The Clinical Classification Software (CCS) is a widely used system for grouping diagnoses and procedures.

Figure 13.9   *Histograms of CCS Procedure Aggregated for Lower and Upper Residual Groups*

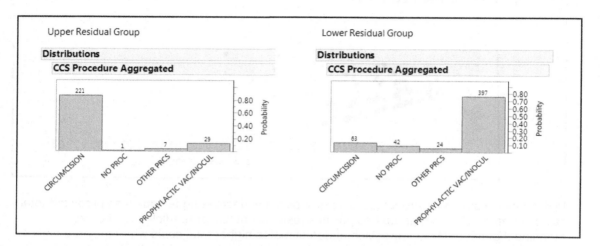

Notice that for the upper residual group circumcision is the dominant procedure while in the lower residual group inoculations are the dominant group. It makes sense that circumcision, a surgical procedure, would have higher costs than vaccinations.

The group of residuals in the higher total cost region is associated with newborns that have complications based on the APR DRG Description. This result is similar to what was discovered from the residual plots of the simple regression analysis with length of stay.

This residual analysis suggests that the model should include predictors that account for different procedures and/or complications.

Assessing Regression Assumptions with Residual Plots

To assess the normality of the residuals, a Normal quantile plot and histogram of the multiple regression residuals were obtained from the Distribution platform as shown in Figure 13.10 on page 217.

Figure 13.10 *Normal Quantile Plot and Histogram of Residuals*

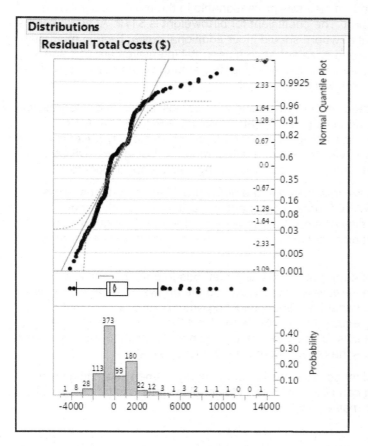

Notice the departure from normality in the large positive residuals. In Figure 13.9 on page 216 we see evidence of non-constant variance. These results are similar to that observed with the simple regression with length of stay.

Analysis Implications

This case has illustrated the basics of multiple regression with two continuous predictors. The multiple regression equation that predicts total costs from length of stay and birthweight showed both independent variables to be significant. However, the addition of birthweight showed only very slight improvement in the goodness-of-fit measures. With a RMSE of $1596, the regression model seems insufficiently precise to be useful in practice. Residual analysis suggests that there are other factors that should be included in the regression model.

Regression coefficients should always be assessed for reasonableness in both direction and magnitude. The coefficient for length of stay seems reasonable in the multiple regression, just as it was in the simple regression. The coefficient for birthweight is $179. At first it seems counterintuitive that a larger weight newborn should incur additional costs. Bear in mind, that CVPH is a Level 1 perinatal center and does not have a neonatal intensive care unit and only handles normal and low-risk births. According to Medline, larger birthweight babies are at risk for injury during delivery and problems with blood sugar.

As a next step, incorporating procedures performed and birth complications into a regression model is indicated. All Patient Refined Diagnosis Related Groups (APR-DRGs), APR severity, and APR risk of mortality data elements could be used which classify patients based on their reason for admission, severity of illness, and risk of morality. Using APR-DRGs to perform analysis relies on complete and accurate encoding by health care providers.

Finally, the data used in this analysis was limited in the detail provided so that individuals could not be identified. The full SPARCS data set has additional information that may improve the model. The length of stay of a newborn is often related to the length of stay of the mother. However, this data set does not allow us to link the records of the newborn and mother.

Multiple linear regression is one of a number of possible methods to obtain predictive models. Model building is often an iterative process requiring the analyst to experiment with different combinations of predictor variables. When selecting among several potential predictive models, all things being equal, it is advisable to select the simplest model (i.e., the one with the fewest predictors). This is referred to as the principle of parsimony. The simplest model should be chosen that meets the required precision for its application.

A good understanding of the problem domain can assist the analyst when searching for good predictors and critically evaluating candidate models. Additional insights can be obtained by consulting the literature or subject matter experts.

Data Definitions

The data definitions can be found in *Inpatient Hospital Discharges (SPARCS De-Identified File): CY 2014 DATA DICTIONARY* which is located in the JMP project ADK_Newborns_2014.jmpprj.

The definitions of the derived data are given in the table below.

Data Element	Description
CCS Procedure Aggregated	Derived from CCS Procedure Description where less common procedures are aggregated into a single category, "OTHER PRCS"

Data Element	Description
Birthweight (lbs)	Newborn birthweight expressed in pounds.

Problems

1 How does gender influence total costs?

    a Conduct a test of hypothesis to determine if there is a difference on average for total costs between males and females?

    b Create a multiple regression that predicts total costs from gender and length of stay. When a nominal variable with two levels is included in a multiple regression two parallel lines are estimated, one for each level. The regression coefficient for the nominal variable represents ½ of the distance between the two lines or one half of the effect of gender on total costs.

    c Compare the difference in the gender mean total costs found in part a with the gender effect (twice the gender regression coefficient) in part b. Why do they differ?

2 The Alice Hyde Medical Center is a 76-bed hospital located in Malone, New York, and is also a part of the University of Vermont Health Network.

    a Create a JMP data table from the file ADK_Newborns_2014.jmp that contains only the data for infants born at the Alice Hyde Medical Center.

    b Conduct two simple regression analyses, one that predicts total costs from length of stay and one that predicts total costs from birthweight (lbs). Compare these regressions to those from the CVPH found in the case "Building a Simple Predictive Model for Health Care Costs for Newborns in Adirondack Hospitals."

    c Perform a multiple regression for the Alice Hyde Medical Center newborn total costs with length of stay and birthweight (lbs) as predictors. Compare your results to those from CVPH found in this case.

3 Select another New York State hospital outside of the Capital/Adirondack health services area and download the data for newborns from SPARCS for 2014. Repeat the analysis of this case and compare your results to those of the Champlain Valley Physicians Hospital.

4 Explore JMP's Partition platform (Analyze > Predictive Modeling > Partition) with the Decision Tree option to predict total costs from the available data in CVPH_Newborns_2014.jmp.

    a How does this method compare to multiple linear regression?

b How do the results compare between the two methods?

References

"Improving Doctors Across New York," Independent Democratic Conference, May 2012, accessed at https://www.nysenate.gov/sites/default/files/REPORT.%20DANY.FINAL %5B1%5D_0.pdf, accessed June 22, 2017.

"Birthweight," MedlinePlus, US National Library of Medicine, https://medlineplus.gov/ birthweight.html, accessed June 25, 2017.

Index

Ready to take your SAS® and JMP® skills up a notch?

Be among the first to know about new books, special events, and exclusive discounts.
support.sas.com/newbooks

Share your expertise. Write a book with SAS.
support.sas.com/publish

sas.com/books
for additional books and resources.

THE POWER TO KNOW.

CPSIA information can be obtained
at www.ICGtesting.com
Printed in the USA
BVOW07s2035301017
499094BV00005B/32/P